STAYING TRUE

*Musings of an Odd-duck Quaker Lesbian
Approaching Death*

Lynn Waddington

PLAIN SPEECH PRESS

PRAYING from the volume *Thirst* by Mary Oliver, published by Beacon Press, Boston. Copyright © 2006 by Mary Oliver, used herewith by permission of the Charlotte Sheedy Literary Agency, Inc.

Definitions found in the glossary are based on the Faith and Practices or Books of Discipline from Mid-America, Ohio Valley, Philadelphia, North Pacific Yearly Meetings of the Religious Society of Friends, and from Janet Hoffman's Testimonies List.

ISBN-13: 978-0-9856492-0-3   ISBN-10: 0985649208
Library of Congress Control Number: 2012940610

Published by Plain Speech Press: Berkeley, CA
www.plainspeechpress.com

Printed and bound in the United States of America

Cover Photo: "Cowboy Lynn" Photo courtesy of Lynn Waddington

For Margaret Sorrel
With Infinite Love

She kept my life running
while I completed
so many of my life's works.

Contents

Gratitudes

I am grateful for my parents: for my mother, Mabel Waddington, who let me be who I am, and for my father, Bill Waddington, for learning to accept that.

I am also grateful for my sister, Mary Waddington, who, when faithful to her own callings, found they came out absolutely true and just right. I am so glad.

My daughter, Kindred, fits her name. She is kindred to all souls. She loves people in a wide-open and trusting way—and they love her. She is also deeply, deeply creative. As I watched her grow up I admired her ability to read what was coming out of her and to gauge the depth, and truth from which it was coming. When what emerges is not of adequate depth Kindred is able to crumple it up and throw it away. That makes all of her work hugely moving and touching, because you recognize it from so deep within yourself. Kindred has been a joy and delight.

I am grateful to my granddaughter, Genevieve, for drawing this story out of me and helping me realize that it is important enough to place out there in the future.

I am deeply grateful to my life companion Margaret Sorrel. I have never known before a relationship with a true soul mate. We are so compatible in our values and assumptions about life, and as we have become more dependent on one another I have seen how our strengths are perfectly complementary. She understands completely. In this time of my final illness I have been leaning on her very strongly to help me get my work out into the world.

I started out believing that I had to work by myself but learned over time that life is about learning to work with others.

I want to thank Cathy Whitmire for having complete faith that these writings were chapters to a book, a book that could be completed despite my having days to live and despite its rough condition. I always felt we could hold hands on either side of the doorway and pass things back and forth. Cathy, you offered me encouragement all along the way, through years, and finally in tugging out the final strands. Your belief in the worthiness of this project, its interest and uniqueness, have kept me going. And your perspectives on its central theme(s) have kept me focused.

I am grateful to Bob Dockhorn, Shellee Davis and Wendy Sanford for their willingness to be manuscript readers. Bob writes in a way that I greatly admire. I also love him because he is a very dear, gentle and easy man. It is hard not to love Bob Dockhorn. Shellee offered me years of fruitful dialogue and feedback on my imagery work in the school of expressive arts during my years of teaching at Sonoma State University. The direction she has taken that work since then is brilliant. I have always admired Wendy's writing and editing skills. I value her gentle wisdom as much as her professional expertise. I entrust this manuscript to each of these readers, knowing that they will each offer loving and helpful touches.

Laurie Wurm's decades of wonderful wrestling with me about God and the place of God in one's life has been greatly helpful and encouraging as my spiritual life has evolved.

Many individual friends served to support me through my many health challenges both informally and through care committees associated with Redwood Forest Friends Meeting, University Friends Meeting and Whidbey Island Worship Group.

I am deeply grateful to Susan Prescott, Robbie Cribbs, Michael Stadler and Tim Clark, each of whom contributed their skills to help the video *When God Was Female* come to fruition.

I trust Margaret, as she shepherds this manuscript to a completed book, to thank those who offered their invaluable assistance after I am no longer here to do so myself.

In love and gratitude for the incredible life I have lived and the mystery of death.

Lynn Waddington
October 2009

Deep gratitude to A.T. Birmingham Young who honored the profound integrity of Lynn's work and, with a light touch, smoothed those places in the manuscript that Lynn would have wished to have further edited. She is an editor nonpareil. She came to know and love Lynn through preparing this book for publication and went far beyond the call of duty in holding my hand through the myriad of details that made possible the pages you now hold.

Appreciation to Gretchen Schlomann for a beautifully designed book, to Susan Prescott for technical assistance throughout, and to Cathy Whitmire for compiling the glossary.

Thanks to the California Institute of Integral Studies who gratefully accepted Lynn's reproductions of female figurines of the Paleolithic and Neolithic eras and the research library that accompanied them. It is a legacy that, like this book, deserves to be studied and enjoyed by people for generations to come.

Thanks to family and friends, near and far, who have waited patiently to hold and read the truth that Lynn so selflessly has shared. Our lives are all the richer for it.

Margaret Sorrel
May 2012

Introduction

When Lynn Waddington first told me about her love of old, hand-carved, wooden jigsaw puzzles, she could not stop smiling. She relished the complexity of every puzzle's unique design, the subtlety of its colors and the imagination of the artist who created it. She loved the puzzles' frustrating trickiness and the challenge of putting each one together. She had a large collection of these puzzles, which she had sought out and carefully curated. She knew that each one was the reflection of a single, unique human being's dreams, artistry and skill.

This book you are holding in your hands, "Staying True," is, similarly, the unique reflection of Lynn's artistry, skill and dreams. Its intricate parts have been carved and fitted with care, colored with honesty, acceptance and, sometimes, painful insight—then polished with joy. She gives us this gift with all of her heart and all of her soul.

As Lynn writes near the end of her life, "What is important now is not the same as at any other time in my life. So I have to let go of preconceptions and listen closely to what my heart wants to do. It wants to make sense of my life, and that's what this writing is about."

"Staying True" is, ultimately, the story of Lynn's spiritual journey. But she knows that one does not mature spiritually without also maturing physically, creatively, emotionally and intellectually. In making "sense" of her life, she wisely includes vivid stories of many personal experiences, from her very early infatuation with the Lone Ranger to her lifelong interest in prehistoric cultures and their depictions of the Divine.

She shares her perceptions of her birth family's joys and hardships with the heartfelt honesty of the child, adolescent or mature daughter and sibling she was at the time. It is clear, on some occasions, that other family members might remember things differently, for Lynn's perspective, even as a child, is that of a "solitary, independent person." "I was so busy protecting myself that my human relationships suffered. They always took a back seat to my spiritual path."

Lynn was born in 1940, into a family of generations of Quakers. Her family lived on the Delaware River, overlooking Delaware Bay, for some years completely without neighbors.

"So most of my time was solitary, unstructured, outdoors. I could make a nest in dry sand, out of the wind, and bake in the sun of early spring. I could hear the footsteps of beetles far away, and the drop of grains of sand as they dried and fell. ... The sound of the waves was a constant breathing, day and night, the moods ranging from the crash of near hurricane to the cat-lapping sounds of a deep fog."

In early adolescence, standing and looking over the Delaware River, Lynn was astounded to realize that, mystically and amazingly, she was completely seen and thoroughly loved by the "most tender love I had ever known."

"Then I noticed a path shooting out from my feet to the horizon, across the river, straight as an arrow.... I wrenched myself out of that altered state and turned away. To my surprise the path now stretched to this new horizon for a moment, before it faded. I saw that I couldn't get away from my path. ... God was present. ... This was not the God I'd been hearing about, even from these intrepid mystics, the Quakers. This God could blow the hat off your head. This God focused in on ME!"

As Lynn seeks to know her path, to be faithful to what she is called to do, she learns from her family, from her dreams, from studying Jungian psychology, from following her intuition, from taking creative risks, and from growing into the truth and safety of her identity as a lesbian woman.

"The truth is, if we want a relationship with God, we need absolute personal integrity."

From mid-life on, Lynn was challenged by illness: Hodgkin's lymphoma, breast cancer and, finally, pulmonary fibrosis. With her partner Margaret Sorrel, Lynn faced death with serenity, humor and acceptance. She was not afraid. She described her final work as "removing, examining, cleaning and reassembling the parts" of her life. She found great joy in this task. At one point, Lynn comments that she was "spinning gold into straw," a wonderful metaphor for the process of taking the treasure of a good life, well remembered, and making everyday sense of both its sadness and its blessings. Lynn knew that having time for such closure was an extraordinary gift. In "Staying True," she has much to teach us about conscious dying.

None of us has been exempt from the stresses of imperfect parenting or being imperfect parents. All of us have stories of illness, missteps, and personal disappointments—in others or in ourselves. Lynn's wisdom about her own life journey has the power to make all of us more sympathetic human beings, whether our challenge is to accept ourselves, to acknowledge another's differing interpretation or different path, or even to forgive what has, until now, seemed unforgivable. Lynn's openness invites us in, extends a hand, so that we feel we are joining her in making sense of her full and rich life.

Her commitment to sharing the truths she has gleaned from her journey makes us want to be more truthful, more observant and more committed to puzzling out our own path more consciously.

From her first years on her beloved Delaware River, to her last years spent in the home she and Margaret built together overlooking Puget Sound—known to Northwest native peoples as the Salish Sea—Lynn worked to stay true to herself. As she wryly notes: "Staying true to oneself is not always a clear path."

"From my home here by the Salish Sea, near the end of my life, I look back up the mountain of my life and see the many gullies the water could have taken to reach the bottom. Mostly I see my choices as influencing the efficiency of my growth toward wholeness. The paths split and come together again, weaving a pattern full of choices, all headed back to the sea, the source."

— Lee Neff

CHAPTER ONE

Unexpected Openings

Cowboy

No Half Measures

Love Coming Through

Fishing for Contact

The Flicker

Saab Story

Unexpected Openings

Cowboy

The last time I visited her, my sister Mary and I spent several days sorting through boxes—no, crates—of slides that we'd unearthed from Mother's house. We threw out all the shots of mountains and made a pile for each of us kids. Yesterday, I finally pulled out my pile and ran them through the projector. Oh, my.

I saw a happy little tomboy in short hair and drag! As my friend Laurie's friend says, "Every one of us comes into this world naked, and after that it's *all* drag." My preferred expression of maleness was the cowboy. Not just any cowboy, mind you. Hopalong Cassidy was ridiculous with his cartoon hat and baggy pants. Gene Autry was a dressed-up city boy who liked to sing. Roy Rogers was a marshmallow. It wasn't 'til the Lone Ranger came along that Hollywood figured out what a cowboy should look like. Well, before that there was Lash LaRue, who sounds like he'd be a fruitcake, but he was actually stunning in all black with a coiled bull whip hanging on his shoulder.

I was limited to the Sears Roebuck selection, but from the pictures I did pretty well. What astounds me now is how supportive my mother was. I'm sure she wasn't comfortable with my expression of self, but by gum, she heard how strong my longing was. She gave me all those haircuts, after all. And I'm sure my measley allowance could never add up to a Sears Roebuck shirt. The only argument I remember her giving me was over cap guns and holsters, and I'm sure that was about the Quaker Peace Testimony. I ended up with them as well. Decades later, when I came out as lesbian to her, she told me she wasn't surprised; she'd guessed as much. I was astounded at that and wondered why I'd waited so long and agonized so much. These slides show me how obvious it was.

Mother not only let me express myself, she also kept Dad at bay. He and I were barely in the same family anyway, but he did have a sharp tongue when he chose. Mother kept that silent. Every Easter (and a few other times as well) I had to don what really felt like drag, right down to the girlish hat. The misery is evident in my face.

I couldn't really become male; I was only playing at it. After all, men had lives of adventure and heroism. Women had lives of housework. The Sears toy section had trucks and six-shooters for boys and stoves and vacuum cleaners for girls. Oh, and dolls. I can remember only one doll: Cynthia, a Betsy Wetsy doll. Pouring a bottle of water in the mouth and immediately changing the wet diaper was a thrill that lasted about a half an hour. Before long I ruined Cynthia forever by feeding her milk instead of water. The Boy Scouts learned knots, fire building, and hiking the wilderness with a compass. The Girl Scouts stitched coin purses with leather thongs in a linoleum-floored room. Who wouldn't want to be a boy?

But what in the world was I going to do about the fact that I was beginning to get crushes, and they were all focused on women and girls? At least this was consistent with my feeling so much like a boy. In order to love a girl, you had to be a boy, didn't you? In the early '50s in rural America, gender options were an iron clad secret. I was a complete oddity, the only person like this in the whole world, evidently. The clothing hadn't kicked up a huge fuss that I was aware of, but the falling in love with my teacher and one or two girlfriends presented a dilemma that I knew I had to work out in secret.

My feelings were in an uproar. Did I know by then how different I was? My lesbian orientation was slow to dawn on me, though it was always there. My parents' marriage was a constant grief to me. I couldn't see choosing to live their life with its tint of dislike and disapproval. I didn't want adult life as it was presented to me. It felt like a violation of my true soul. I felt there was no place for me.

One day early in adolescence I took my dilemma outside to the front yard, and as I stood looking over my beloved Delaware River I felt the calm seep into me as it usually did. And then I was wrenched open. All of a sudden, I was halted in my tracks. I realized I was trembling and crying. Sweat was running down my sides.

I was seen through and through. I was translucent like a window pane. Every flaw of my being was visible, but the fear that brought was dissolved by the sweetest, most tender love I had ever known. I was seen and I was loved exactly for what was seen.

I was accepted with a deep and tender love.

This was God—who saw me uniquely and bent down to touch me alone.

Then I noticed a path shooting out from my feet to the horizon, across the river, straight as an arrow, kind of lit up. This part was too strange for comfort. I wrenched myself out of that altered state and turned away. To my surprise the path now stretched to this new horizon for a moment, before it faded. I saw that I couldn't get away from my path. I broke the "spell," shook myself back to normal reality. I found a place to sit and just felt it for a long time before I was able to go indoors again.

How can I describe these moments? There's no language for it. God was present, and I was aware of Her/Him. I was standing in another world, still here in this place, but in a world that was made of pure energy. It was focused on me, specifically. I was seen, through and through, as naked as glass. With that terrifying vulnerability though came love such as I've never known. I was loved for exactly who I was. I trembled with the force of it.

This was not the God I'd been hearing about, even from these intrepid mystics, the Quakers. This God could blow the hat off your head. This God focused in on ME! Not us/humankind or even this group doing worthy work. This God bothered to say I was OK as I was. More, that I had somewhere to go and, presumably, something to do. Perhaps far from this region where I was such an oddity. And even though I hadn't a clue, the way was clear as day. It was, in fact, impossible to get off my path! If God had been tuning in on my dilemma all along, S/He would continue to be with me, watching out for me, loving me.

Perhaps I would be able to live my life without lying and hiding, without splitting myself in two; the acceptable working in the world, the unacceptable privately flooding me with shame. I couldn't see this happening in the South Jersey marshlands, but I would someday head for the far horizon, and that might be a different story.

I carried the secret of my attractions for many years, more than ten, before I told anyone. But I pondered the message of the path and found it vastly reassuring. It was clear that I was OK as I was. I was to stay true to myself. I was to trust where I was led and do what I had to do.

More than that, God existed. God was somehow aware of me and cared about me. I might be different, but that didn't make me wrong. Perhaps that uniqueness was the heart of what God wanted me to contribute, farther down the path.

No Half Measures

At one point after my mystical experience on the lawn I considered entering a convent. Isn't that where mystics go? The structure would surely help me build a spiritual discipline and find outlets in the world for my willing hands. I liked that it would remove pressure to marry or train for a profession and then compete in the fierce world.

The obstacles were many though. I'd never been in a Catholic church, for one. I'd never met a nun. Catholicism seemed an extreme opposite from Quakerism. And while I did have a pious side, I also had playful, lustful, and creative sides. Could I be faithful to my own experience and understanding of God while being faithful to the Church? Joan of Arc didn't fare so well.

That desire faded, or rather became a symbol for something I wanted to create for myself. Occasionally the local Quakers would pull out of their bureau drawers the long skirts and bonnets, the britches and lapel-less coats that were the Quaker habits of an earlier time. We become docents in a living history exhibit at our old meetinghouses. I loved these times. The Quaker gray expressed my inner faithfulness, my own quirky form of nun. This was my heritage. There were twelve or thirteen generations of Quakers in my blood, stretching back through the days when Quakers had to marry Quakers or be disowned.

At times it felt like everything I needed was right here in my own roots. And who could ask for more than a core adherence to God's continuing revelation? Not to the authors of the Bible, and not to some church father, but to the still, small voice within myself. The founding couple of Quakerism in the 1600s had an exchange that sits at the core of my faith. Margaret Fell was blown away when she heard George Fox say, "Jesus saith this, and the apostles say this, but what canst thou say? And is it inwardly of God?"

So we are called to be mystics, to stand as tall, perhaps, as the Old Testament prophets, to go for the direct experience, not the theological study of others' experiences. And then we are called to live a life in accord with what is being revealed to us. Another founder of the Quaker movement wrestled mightily with his ongoing sins. When he gets around to naming them, they are his inability to live his convictions. He is convinced that God dwells equally within all people, and yet he wears the symbolic trappings of privilege in his aristocratic clothing and behavior. He knows what an uproar it will cause to wear "Quaker plain" and to refuse to bow and address others with their fancy titles.

What a tall order, to lay down my own privilege, to live true to what was revealed to me, to put myself in God's hands. It's been a worthy challenge that's excited and inspired me. And I've felt like a failure in this task all my life.

Most writings about following a leading describe a careful discerning process. I was supposed to meditate or pray on the problem, and when a possibility presented itself, I was to call together others to reflect with me on whether this was indeed the right move. At times I didn't do any of that—those times when I was so clear in my heart that I didn't want others to pile on reasons of the head why my course might be wise or unwise. The trembling vision of rightness was as powerful as any of my mystical experiences had been.

Knowing what is the right thing to do is something I believe we all share. Sometimes it flits through our awareness almost subliminally. I believe it is a talent or skill we're meant to develop, like remembering our dreams. In both cases we have to pay attention and give it a place of honor to be rewarded with its gifts. The more we write down our dreams, reread them and try to make sense of them, the more clear and elaborate they become. And the more we act on our inner sense of rightness, the more loudly and clearly it will speak to us.

Of course, acting on the "still, small voice" can be terrifying. It can rip apart the fabric of our lives and throw us into the unknown. But I tell you, life won't be boring. Help is there when we rely on it for our very lives. It doesn't work so well to try to live a faithful life in half measures. Once we've activated that inner voice, it will haunt us the whole time we're trying to ignore it.

I don't want this to sound too black and white, though. Missed opportunities come around again in another form, and which one we pick up on can feel almost arbitrary. From my home here by the Salish Sea, near the end of my life, I look back up the mountain of my life and see the many gullies the water could have taken to reach the bottom.

Mostly I see my choices as influencing the efficiency of my growth toward wholeness. The paths split and come together again, weaving a pattern full of choices, all headed back to the sea, the source.

Many of the opportunities I passed on would have taken me away from what's been most true, and that true path has been difficult to name.

Love Coming Through

In my Quaker upbringing, the core belief was that I was under God's care in a very direct way. When I stole my brother's wallet (temporarily, I told myself, to teach him a lesson and make him sweat), afterwards my mother outlined for me very vividly what that must feel like to him. I was sent up to my room to make peace with my conscience, to listen for what God wanted me to do to make things right. There was no yelling or spanking, no Bible verses to read. I used the time to play with paper dolls, though my mind continued to mutter and muse on the situation.

God was assumed to be present. Quakers affirm that there is that of God in everyone and base their practices on that assumption. Based in silence, a worship service is designed to first listen for "the still, small voice," and then for anyone present to give voice to the things that emerge with some potency, that make one "quake." As a child I grew used to quieting myself. We were allowed to swing our feet, for example. It made the old bench rock back and forth, but our family filled up that bench and rode out each youngster's fidgety phase. I can remember my full-yet-idle mind studying the wood grain on the bench in front of me, so much like swirling water and waves. The ancient carpet had a repeating pattern of what I now recognize as mandalas. At the time, my eyes traveled the lines of the maze, in and out, part square part circle.

After the first twenty minutes or so of silence, someone was likely to say something. These messages occasionally gave me food for thought or blended in with my own thoughts, and some gave me practice in the craft of tuning them out. Then at one particular Meeting in my early adolescence, I found myself wrestling with real issues in my life. I can't remember them now, only what happened. I came to a brick wall; there was no way out of my dilemma. I became profoundly depressed. And then someone rose and spoke directly to that issue—directly to me. It was as if she had heard my whole sequence of thoughts. The depression lifted, I breathed deeply and moved forward—until I came to another dilemma. Amazingly enough, someone rose and spoke directly to that! On the way home I casually asked my folks if it had been a special Meeting for them, and from their response I could tell it hadn't. Those messages were meant for me. And maybe some of the dull messages in other Meetings were not dull for someone else. Who was listening in to our thoughts? Who was really speaking through these people?

A Meeting for Worship could certainly bring piercing clarity—for the word of God has only human voices to express itself. I was at that time of life when I saw how poorly I fit into the society around me. I wanted to take my artist's vision beyond the local women's club and county fair. I didn't want to become a farmer's wife. In fact, I didn't want to become anybody's wife. My budding sexuality was leading me more toward girls than boys. This was completely unknown territory. There were no examples, no words or labels for this variety of human experience. This was the early '50s and a conservative, rural area. I can remember the uproar caused by my kissing a girl on the mouth on the school bus. Mother had to explain to me that I shouldn't do that. I accepted it but didn't understand it at all.

Fishing for Contact

Laurie, my lesbian Episcopal priest friend, gave me a wonderful image about God in our lives. We go fishing for that contact with a fishing pole, when the contact is really a whale. She talked about the whale-watching trip she went on. She expected the powerful tail and flukes rearing dramatically out of the water, like you see on TV and in magazines. When the other passengers rushed to the side pointing, she saw nothing but empty sea, huge and flat. After a while she became aware of a vast whiteness under the boat. It was there under them, rolled over, belly up. Obviously very aware of them.

It's a delightful image, both halves, the puny fishing pole and the subtlety of the underlying support. But in both those images, God is other, elsewhere. When I feel Her presence it permeates everything: me, the beautiful world in front of me, my community of loved ones, my past and future. I lose my boundaries. I feel peaceful, loved, and loving.

The Flicker

I know what the Mystics and Saints mean by "God." They've experienced the awe and love also. Without that experience it's easy to argue that the notion of a God is childish, illogical, contradictory, unnecessary—it becomes a philosophical construct, open to debate. Like love, like orgasm, like the Grand Canyon, it has to be experienced.

Even Mother Teresa spent her life a spiritual agnostic, searching for a divine response. This search is the quest of our times, and perhaps of all times. Perhaps we build cathedrals and go on crusades not because we've found, but are seeking to find. Who, then, has known certainty? And those of us who've glimpsed it for a moment, how well can we carry that memory with us, and for how long? How brittle, how rigid does that fleeting certainty become over time, if it doesn't fade away?

These times that we live in are marked by honesty. I like that people are naming and living in their spiritual truth. I'm not at all distressed by the number of atheists and agnostics among us, or the number who take their Sunday morning service in a little fishing boat. This is an honest search, an honoring of what brings peace and oneness with the natural world. These peaceful hours in the fishing boat, or the garden, or the hiking trail may be the most common kind of church service we have today.

The Quakers of that first radical generation asked what you knew from your experience of God, not what others experienced, or what you or others thought about God. Those thoughts were tossed off as "airy notions," a snare to beware of. But the experience—ah, that was a rich gold mine that could change your life beyond recognition. These were the things worth speaking about.

In fact, if we could only speak of these things, we could begin to build a religion without dogma, one made up of all our glimpses of the Divine. I imagine it would have no sectarian differences. I imagine we would find that we are all of a single family. What a solid foundation upon which to build community and weave a just and compassionate society.

But all this depends on having the experiences, and most people imagine Jacob wrestling with the angel and think, "I've never had anything like that." No, that's very rare. What's more common is the tiny flicker of conscience that comes and goes in a moment.

In the '90s, my partner Margaret and I lived in Seattle, next to a playfield with benches and bathrooms and shade trees. It was a favorite place to park for people who had only a car to live in. They generally moved elsewhere during the day. They were mostly quiet and tidy neighbors. There was one woman who caught at my heart. I could see myself in her. Why was I warm and comfortable on this side of the wall, and she cold and cramped and hungry on that side? The flicker of conscience wanted to reach out to her. I wanted so much to offer her a shower, to invite her to breakfast. Our boys had left and their bedrooms in the basement were used only for visits.

But to open my home—our home—to her was fraught with dangers. Did she struggle with drugs or mental stability? Would our most beloved things be safe? I detested this miserly clutching and teetered on the brink of a Gandhian leap into the open air of how things should be. Instead I argued with the flickers. I waved and said Hi. When our garden started producing, I took her a little bag of tomatoes.

The flickers never let up. How might they inform my life?

So many friends seem to find living in the quest, in the question, to be agonizing. They collect belief systems the way others collect antiques or art, and bury their tiny flickerings of spirit in a barrage of chakras, spirit guides, heavenly realms—a swirling storm of "airy notions." Wouldn't it be more useful to hold on to that humble, little flicker?

I know, it feels inadequate in the face of these sophisticated cosmologies. Is this all there is? Some people have big, beautiful mystical experiences. Some have vast, intelligent structures, but, for them, this little flicker doesn't answer anything. It isn't enough to build a life on, is it? What's the message? What do I do now?

The most radically useful passage in the Bible for me has been "God is love." But it's still so full of questions. When I love, is that God loving through me? Am I experiencing God when I love, or when I'm loved? Did Mother Teresa pour God over India in copious floods all her life without recognizing the God flowing through her? How can that be?

If love so seldom feels like God's presence, is it our love that's somehow inadequate or our recognition of its divine nature? Is it better for us to ignore the God part entirely, so we don't begin to feel God-like ourselves? Yet miracles have flowed from the hands of loving, naive believers.

What kinds of miracles can flow from *these* hands? That's the question. With my tiny flicker, what can I do that would be faithful? Those little flickers leave such inadequate instructions! I can run and join worthy causes, but do they have anything to do with the flicker? Without putting these brief connections to use somehow, haven't I missed the point entirely?

Sometimes one of those causes catches hold and it feels like, "Here your talents are well used." Other times, the busyness feels like it's covering up, crowding out, the space that might reveal what these hands could do. Ah, the faith it takes to stop and listen at those times! Everyone is still clamoring at your door, "Stay faithful to *us*! We need you!" And what does the flicker say? Most likely nothing. The devil of it is that God speaks when She pleases, rather than when we need it. What kind of a religion is that?

And yet the flicker often makes a comment on our decisions, or on the crowded results of our decisions. I often can't tell if a thing is right until after I've tried it and see how it impacts my life. If I'm not careful, I've already made some kind of commitment by then, so it becomes important at beginnings to state carefully the truth about my tentativeness.

There is, within the Quaker concern for speaking truth, a tradition of careful language that is hard for my impulsive nature to practice. My grandmother always replied to my exaggerations with the quote, "If it were more, I'm sure thee would have said so." The saintly John Woolman was known for his impeccable honesty, so much so that, according to an apocryphal story, his rascally son and his best friend determined to catch him out. The friend came to the door and asked John if his son was there.

He had been innocently reading in the living room, but scampered out the window as his father went to the door. But John was not so easily caught. He answered to the friend, "He was in the living room when I left it."

Can I learn to apply that kind of careful language to my decisions? "Let me ponder this and get back to you. It feels important, but I may have to stop doing something else to comfortably fit this in, or it may not sit well with me over time." The discernment process is really to see if a flicker of yes or no will appear. When the No comes, we need to lay that activity down.

It seems like the gaps between flickers is huge, but really it's quite natural to keep a listening ear, to ask, "is this right?" in much the same way those of an earlier time said "God willing" in mid-sentence and meant it. I struggle to welcome the sleepless nights and uneasy heart that signal that this deep communication with God must be rumbling in my depths. God still drags the couch across the living room floor as She did during those long-ago thunderstorms, but now it happens deep within.

That's where the secular humanism steps in. We have such huge gaps of "in the meantime..." that we need to fill them with compassionate, ethical treatment of those around us. This is the time for us to become the people we would have us be. And to do it in the face of a daily culture that subverts this impulse at every step. Loving-kindness? Honesty? Humility? Generosity? Slow thoughtfulness? These are all radical in the workplace and in our daily lives.

What helps heed the flickers? Our move to the country has helped. Our settling on less income helps. The strong neighborhood community we luckily fell into helps.

Saab Story

There are occasional times when God yells Her communication, times when a flicker would be entirely insufficient. When I was living in San Francisco, I had an accident on the freeway in Marin County in my Saab. It left me okay but my car was pretty wrecked. I had the fender pried away from the tire and decided to drive it to Berkeley, to the only Saab mechanics in the Bay area at the time. As I was crossing the Bay Bridge, which has no breakdown lane, in the middle of the evening rush hour, I realized that the hood was unsecured. These early Saabs had a hood that hinged at the front end and lifted near the windshield. Gusts of wind were briefly lifting the hood up to obscure my view. I saw disaster ahead, for me and other hapless commuters, as I approached the middle of the bay where wind might be stronger and steadier. I prayed "Oh God, what do I do?" I got an immediate answer of "Wind down your window!" I could almost hear the "stupid" attached to the end. I hastened to obey, just in time to catch the hood as it lifted off in a big gust. I could just reach by stretching way out the window. I managed to keep my grip across the bridge until I could pull over on the other side to wedge it down with a bottle of suntan lotion. I was shaken and humbled and grateful. I was completely surprised by having my prayer answered so immediately. I don't really believe in intercessory prayer and had never recognized my earlier calls for help as prayer.

CHAPTER TWO

Working Toward Adulthood

Working Toward Adulthood

Making Sense of a Life at Sixty

I thought I'd put down my reflections on my life so far, at this sixtieth year mark. It seems an ideal time, being far enough along to have a critical mass to ponder, and still enough of my wits left to do the pondering. Catch it quick. My mother never caught the moment. I'm beginning this in July, after a month or so in my childhood home, Salem Cove, South Jersey, so a certain *ambiance* of my early life is still fresh, at least the hot and muggy part.

I was born in 1940. My Quaker parents were homesteading in a derelict duck-hunting lodge called "the Round House" because of its peculiar octagonal shape. It was a quarter-mile off a remote road and without any twentieth-century amenities. It was on the Delaware River waterfront just above the bay, where the far shore was three or four miles away. It was completely without neighbors for many years. The wildness of this setting lives deep in my soul.

Summers were a waterfront paradise. We seemed to live in bathing suits from May to September. Mother put a bucket by the door to dip our feet—and sometimes our butts—into before entering the house. Low tide gave us a hundred feet of shallow water on the mud flats and fifty feet of dry sand to play in, and this extended to either side farther than we wanted to go. In one direction was the point, at the mouth of the Salem River, and in the other direction was the long sweep of Salem Cove. The country club was a short hike away, and beyond that were cottages. But right around us was wild for many years.

The Round House was designed for seasonal occupation, no insulation, cracks all over the place. Once I followed an odd sound to find it was loose linoleum flapping in the breeze that whistled through a crack in the wall. On cold mornings Mother lit up the pot-bellied stove, hung our clothes around it, and ringed it with chairs before calling us out of our beds. Up on the chairs out of the wicked draft, we could just endure that stripped-down moment between pajamas and clothes. The outhouse was right outside the kitchen—cold, stinky, and full of spiders.

I was too young to remember the year the river froze over. Mother and Dad stacked me and Mary and Bill—three and four years older—onto the sled and pulled us far out onto the ice. But when the creaking and groaning of the ice signaled its breaking up on the high tide, they had to run for shore with us in tow. Family legend has it that they leapt a widening gap, yanking us in an arc over the water, in order to reach shore. We never saw a freeze like that again.

Those early years hold many family legends beyond my memory and some fragments that stuck. I remember Mother hanging laundry out in the winter, when bluejeans froze stiff long before they dried. I remember feeding the cantankerous old red hen and the time she jumped on my arm and pecked at my eye. My flinch saved my sight and gave me a hole in the eyebrow. Mother chased that hen down with an axe. I believe that was the end of my fantasies of a life as a farmer or a farmer's wife.

To Mary and Bill I was a tagalong, too young to be any fun. They once defined a jail by pacing off a square from tree to bush, then locked me inside with a "Tick-double lock!" I'm not sure how much I believed the magic ritual and how much I just hated being excluded. Mother found me crying inside the jail and released me with another "Tick-double lock." The imaginary world was very much a part of the material world.

So most of my time was solitary, unstructured, outdoors. I could make a nest in dry sand, out of the wind, and bake in the sun of early spring. I could hear the footsteps of beetles far away, and the drop of grains of sand as they dried and fell. I could smell the mud of the meadows emerging as the tide fell. The sound of the waves was a constant breathing, day and night, the moods ranging from the crash of near hurricane to the cat-lapping sounds of a deep fog.

This was my first and most primal religion. I was a part of the warm and caring natural world that held me in its hand. Though fundamentally benign, the natural world was also lethal, unpredictable, and impartial.

A humbling experience. I was clearly not in control, nor were any other human beings. Nature seemed a vast, interconnected network of events. I was the equivalent of a beetle or a tree, part of the web and just as expendable. I loved to ponder the bug that was exploring my hairy arm, pretend to be her size, making my way through thick brush.

This natural religion merged perfectly with our formal religion. As Quakers, we sat in silence every Sunday to ponder our lives and feel the divine presence—activities beyond me as a small child, and yet not really beyond me at all. It was the same as lying in the nest of sand, only more uncomfortable. I traveled the pattern in the carpet with my eyes as if I were walking a labyrinth. I swung my feet or ran my finger round and round a button, and just existed in time.

The family did very well as a nurturing entity. We fused together because of our isolation. For the most part, everyone was treated with love and respect, and encouraged to be true to ourselves and creative. The ugly thorn in the midst of this was therefore doubly hard to understand. It wasn't until I was forty-five that I knew why my father treated my mother and me with contempt.

I was not his child. I was the product of his father's visit and rape of my mother. This secret broke my parents' love and trust and poisoned their marriage. He would never let her talk about it. In fact, his one moment of physical abuse was slugging her for trying to insist that they talk it out. He preferred to blame her, as if she had cuckolded him. He spoke to her with scathing contempt from that point on, even in simple, innocent matters.

He also treated me as someone else's child for many years, though gradually he accepted me into the family. As far back as I can remember things, we seemed to be only prickly and uneasy with each other. I was smarter and handier with tools than he was, and I always figured I was too flip with him when his facts were wrong, or when he'd try to loosen a nut on my bike by turning it the wrong way. My biggest grudge with him was how he treated Mother, who was, after all, my champion.

Mother was an artist, a free spirit, who had one year of Philadelphia College of Art before reluctantly going into nurse's training. She painted always; I think it kept her sane. She also built cupboards or whatever else was needed. Dad's art forms were stone masonry and humor. He built sea walls and steps to the beach, terraces and fireplaces. He loved to mix up a wheelbarrow full of cement.

My dad was the core of the Quaker Meeting, the equivalent of the pastor in a worship service void of program. His teasing humor and wry images endeared him to everyone. When we played "I'm going to Grandma's and I'm going to take . . ." he would add things like "a collapsible, reinforced, agate commode," or "a pink laminated toothbrush with a monogrammed handle." He'd say that someone ran like a bag of hammers. That the name Ralph sounded like a belch in an empty ice tea glass.

Time seemed very different to me then, perhaps to all of us. Without radio and television, without neighbors, committees, and organized activities, time was as large a gift as air or sunlight. We complained of boredom, but we also knew that it was up to us to fill or use that time. Studying nature, doing useful projects, make believe and creativity were our play.

I carved seals and jeeps out of bars of soap. I drew rearing horses and seascapes with charcoal—good sticks of artists' charcoal—on the want ads, a wonderful canvas with mottled gray background. I invented useful things like self-greasing frying pans. And I constructed an elaborate full-size Native American teepee following the instructions on the dividers in the Shredded Wheat box, complete with a fish rack and a turning spit over the fire ring. I lived there for much of one summer.

One Christmas my parents bought me a National Geographic book called *Everyday Life in Ancient Times*. It opened a lifelong fascination with ancient and prehistoric cultures. I wanted to know how others had lived, what was normal for them. I was fascinated with archaeology and ancient civilizations. I loved seeing the safety pin that was invented several thousand years before Christ, and the leaping bull dancers of Crete. I realized these inventors were as smart as I, just dealing with a different set of problems to solve. My world expanded in time before it expanded in space. New York City might as well have been on another planet.

Through my school years we gradually accumulated neighbors, whose summer cottages became year-round homes. A road came through and with it electricity and phone. We cut down a tree, dug a basement-size hole, and put up a cinder block house with fireplaces in the living room and the basement. Anticipating the fire, I climbed into the fireplace—there was almost nothing else built—curled into a tight log and blazed. I was chanting "Burn, burn . . ." as I pictured the flames transforming my body into heat and ash. It was magnificent, until Mary and Bill discovered me and danced around hooting with laughter and chanting "Burn, burn . . ." I can't remember the tempo of my chant because that was lost in the ridicule. But the image of a large piece of ash flaking from my body is still a memory. Much later someone asked me if I thought this was my first true mystical experience, and I could let go of the humiliation enough to restore the awe.

I knew I was a good swimmer. I'd tested myself once for distance and given up in boredom at five miles. I'd tested my lung capacity by drifting along the bottom until I reached euphoria. I knew that was the signal to surface, but I treasured those moments of blissful oneness with the river.

The day I turned ten, an off-shore hurricane flooded all the roads. We had to evacuate. I remember poling the boat down the road and asking if this meant I couldn't have my birthday party. Another year I watched a parade of bathtubs and front porches go by. Hurricanes were such a source of philosophical insight. They brought a level of real life I don't have to deal with much anymore. We sat on a roof one time and watched a man in a tiny sailboat go under. He was too flustered to lower his sail. We could hear him calling "Ahoy!" but the Coast Guard wasn't going anywhere in that storm. He disappeared behind the waves several times, then appeared sideways, his sail caught in the wave. He called "Ahoy!" again, appeared again, and then disappeared. Helpless on the roof, we grieved him.

Another time I stood in the front yard leaning back on the force of the wind. I was looking out over the raging river when the stump of a large limb sailed past my head. The branches knocked me down. I watched the limb sail out over the water so fast it didn't sink toward the water for a long time. I could have been impaled on the leading end of it. My mother could lose a child as easily as the tree lost the limb. I saw that it was dumb to stand in such an unsheltered place at a time like that. I didn't see that I was saved by God for some reason.

As neighbors moved in, we had to learn the ways of small-town life. A gang of kids accumulated in the Cove, all younger than I, but closer to playmates than anything I'd known so far. I "youthened" myself to play with them, but nowhere near as much as I had to in order to play with my little sister—six years younger. Jeanne and I found little to do together but march endlessly around the rug to the tune of *The March of the Wooden Soldiers.*

This gang had more differences with me than age. Culturally they were completely alien. Down at the point the boys played at humping the only other girl, while I watched and declined to participate. One brother and sister were quite knowledgeable since they slept in a one-room converted garage with only a blanket hung between them and their parents. When puberty struck, the whole gang insisted on seeing my pubic hair and breasts. They finally cornered me in my upstairs bedroom and made me lower my pants. Then there was my trusted neighbor with a disability, Charlie, who sexually exploited me. Where were my parents when I needed them?

A neighbor's son returned home from a stint in the Army with a sizeable collection of pornography, images that burned into my brain indelibly. He later tied up a litter of our kittens in a gunny sack, tossed them in the river, and shot at them until they sank. I sobbed this story to my mother, an old friend of his mother. A few days later, his mother called me on the carpet and tried to make me retract the story. She kept saying, "You know you're lying. He wouldn't do a thing like that." This encounter upset me even more than the drowning itself.

Dad Versus Father

In my mid-40s, while I was living near my family, I drove my mother in to town for some thrift store shopping. She wanted to tell me something, but it was a struggle for her. I pulled over to the curb and gave her all my focus. The story that came out was about my conception. My dad, who'd always had a rocky relationship with me, was not my father. His dad was.

Now his dad was a real renegade, notorious for his trips down the Chesapeake in his boat with his secretary and a case of fine liquor. He took a shine to my mother. One day when Dad was asleep upstairs from working the night shift, he forced himself on her. "He compromised me," was how she worded it. She called out for my dad. His father clamped his hand over her mouth and nose and continued. She heard Dad get out of bed, cross the floor, and come down the stairs. This old house was full of creaky boards. She thought, "Good, he'll rescue me."

But he didn't. He got far enough to watch, she was sure, but he couldn't stop it. When they were first married he'd come out with a very un-pacifist statement, unfitting for a Quaker, which had surprised her: "If anybody lays a hand on you, I'll kill him." It's likely he'd been referring to his father. They never talked about that day. It ruined their marriage.

Mother became pregnant from that encounter, and I was the result. From the beginning my "dad" treated me like some neighbor's kid. Mother would watch him playing in the yard with the older two while I stood and watched from the sidelines. She'd step out and insist he give me a turn.

He treated Mother with contempt the whole time I knew them. Once, when she was very ill and lying on the rug, she asked him to fetch her coat to use as a blanket. He gave her a long indignant look, then threw the coat in her direction and left. She crawled over to get it. He was loving and thoughtful to those in the community, and well loved. At home, though, there was no escaping his contempt for her.

I seethed with outrage on her behalf all my life. She was my constant champion, and I wanted to be hers. It wasn't until he was on his deathbed, made mute and bed-bound by a massive stroke that I knew I couldn't put it off any longer. I knew the story now and it softened my anger. We'd heard from a cousin that Dad's father had possibly molested Dad's sister, or sisters. Dad may well have known and been powerless to stop the abuse.

I saw what a bind he was in if watching powerless had become a habit. He hadn't killed his father. Nor had he carried on any of his father's bad behavior. He'd lived a good life. As oldest son, he stepped in to bring in some money and hold things together. He did this as a teen, at the price of a higher education. His personality called out for him to be a teacher, a historian, a philosopher. Instead he was a laborer and then a salesman. He never in his life had a job that was right for him.

People said of his father that he was much better than *his* father. So Dad had halted that nasty heritage as much as he could. I found a new respect for him I'd never felt before. I was ready to talk to him about this huge taboo skeleton in the closet. His stroke meant he couldn't leave. He had to listen.

I asked my siblings to guard the door. I entered with fear and trembling. God, this was hard. This was the very thing I'd been most afraid of, confronting him. Was there still too much fury in me, enough to blow him away? I knew I didn't want to do that, yet stifling it might shut me up completely, turn it inward and into tears.

One thing I've learned is that tears are not my friend. They're too cowardly. They rush in to stop up my mouth. So I've grown somewhat inured to the embarrassment of tears in my voice, on my face.

I sat on the edge of his bed and told him why I was there. He looked away but stayed alert to every word. I reconstructed the scene and said I thought I understood why he'd been unable to stop his father. What I blamed him for was not that, but for making Mother bear the brunt of his outrage. I debunked the myth of his generation, that a woman couldn't be raped against her will.

I debunked his assumption that she had invited or wanted his father's attentions. I knew she despised that man. Her tears at his funeral were of relief, not of grief. How different their marriage would have been if he'd comforted her rather than blamed her. She hadn't deserved his contempt for all these years.

I said if he wanted to go with a peaceful soul he had to make things right with her. Knowing that he couldn't speak, I said I didn't think it would take much. If he held her hand and looked into her eyes she'd know he loved her. When I asked his permission to tell Mother about this conversation he gave a huge and deliberate nod. When I asked if he'd like me to send her in to see him he shook his head. I understood there was a lot to think about.

Mother was a little addled by this time. I hoped it wasn't too late for her to benefit. Even though I told her of the conversation, she still came to me a day or two later looking baffled. He'd gripped her hand so hard it hurt, and seemed to be pleading with her, but what was the question? I had to tell her the whole story of the conversation again. I suggested she visit him again and offer him some words that he could nod to. She did go back in, but I didn't hear much about it. I did feel clear that my job was complete. I walked down the beach and let fifty years of weight slide off my shoulders.

The Burn

Grandmother and Granddad Pancoast, on my mother's side, lived on into my youth, though they were old enough that I didn't get much of a firsthand impression. They seemed quiet, turned inward. Granddad was slowed by Parkinson's. They were always together and solicitous of each other. They were much in love, all through their life.

Mary was the only daughter of a wealthy and influential Quaker druggist in Philadelphia. Leonidas was a country Quaker boy. They met when she visited her country cousins. I have a photo of them in their courting days. Her dress is about as elaborate as a Quaker can get away with, and her hat was clearly pushing the limit. She had a weakness for hats. He is in a handmade suit whose seams are a little puckery. They're blissfully happy.

When my mother was five or so tragedy struck the family. She was upstairs helping her mother make beds when they both heard her father call from outside, "Mary?" Her mother replied, "Just a minute, Leo." He repeated "Mary" in a way that alerted Mary. They both went to the window and saw Leo standing there on fire. His clothing, his hair. He looked up at their window and Mother saw his blackened hair slide off the back of his head. Mary ran down and smothered the fire.

He had climbed down a dry well with his lantern to fix something when the flame ignited a gas leak and exploded. My Uncle Ben was holding the top of the ladder and peering in. He was blown back against the barn wall and knocked unconscious.

Granddad's walk to the house gave him third-degree burns over most of his body. Nobody gave him a chance of surviving.

I'm sure it was Mary's father who sent the specialist down to the farm, a doctor with extensive burn experience from the First World War. It was also he, I'm sure, who hired a couple to nurse him and run the household. Baby Edward had just been born, the sixth child. Mary sat by Leo's bedside in the kitchen and left Edward in his cradle just outside the doorway. Edward didn't survive his first year. But Leo did.

The Philadelphia doctor prescribed an almost constant bathing with tea. The tannic acid soothed and protected his new skin. Leo lay naked on a tightly stretched body-length rubber sheet which funneled the run-off rivulets of tea into buckets. His top sheet was baked in the oven to sterilize it, and hung suspended over his body. The children tip-toed around and did their chores without fuss.

It took years, but Leo recovered. They sold the farm and moved to town. He took work as an accountant. They had two more children. I don't remember any scars on his face. I don't remember seeing any other part of his body, even on our beach in the summer.

Mother remembers those years as a time when they lived on biscuits and gravy. There was flour and there was lard. Lots of flour and you have biscuits; lots of lard and you have gravy. And then from relatives, neighbors, and members of Quaker Meeting came anonymous gifts of food left on the porch, sometimes whole bushels of potatoes, peaches, and corn. Grandmother sold off her heirlooms one by one, with very few exceptions, two of which live now in my home; I am unable to part with the cut glass bowl and the china tea set.

Philandering Father

I know surprisingly little about my paternal grandparents. Bill Sr. (my biological father) died while I was still in the womb and Edith died soon after.

Bill was, as near as I can see, the playboy son of a wealthy family. His father was a wholesaler in a little port town, and, by all reports, a swaggering, misogynistic (and Quaker), pillar of the community.

Bill married Edith, a sweet girl from a good Quaker family. (At least half the town was Quaker in those days.) Their marriage embodied the power imbalance and cruelty typical of turn-of-the-century relations as thoroughly as Leo and Mary embodied the rare mutual respect and playfulness of true love.

As a father himself, Bill Sr. hated to be tied down. Responsibility was no fun. His primary love was his boat, and it was a beauty. There are pictures with Edith aboard, and with his daughters, but the stories that got passed down are of his trips with other women, and a galley full of whiskey.

As I said, this man was not my grandfather, but my biological father. His blood runs unfiltered through my veins. My siblings got his genes tempered by Edith's rather saintly genes. They stay put and work things out, even in difficult circumstances. I dump a bad scene and move on. My path is littered with relationships that didn't work out, good times that went a bit over the line, and rebellions against responsibility.

Who knows if genes are the carriers of personality. Something is, I'm sure. I carry Bill Sr. in me whether I like it or not, whether I knew him personally or not. It's my job in this life to reconcile those bloodlines, to mingle them in a way that transforms the bad into a better way of being. In me, Leo and Bill Sr. must duke it out.

They appear in many guises in my dreams, where over the years I've watched their slow transformation. And they each get projected onto the hapless men in my life, who also transform these genetic ghosts through their honest interactions with me.

This has been the work of a lifetime. Perhaps therapy could have sped it up, but paying close attention to my dreams has worked very well for me. Especially going back over a lot of time to pull out a particular thread, like *men*. Early dreams have threatening, out-of-control soldiers shooting at each other, while I try to stay safely out of their way to carry on some semblance of my own life. In another version I desperately try to send out a signal from the heavily fortified headquarters of some evil despot. I can see where I'd have benefited from some kind of normal relationship with my Dad.

Over time the men of my dreams become slowly less of a threat and more of a help. I won't take you on that whole journey, but now the men of my dreams are likable, easygoing friends and helpers. An incredible transformation. Likewise, in my life I enact less and less of Bill Sr. I've found Leo coming out more, his dry humor and loving steadfastness. This is through no effort of mine. It has seemed to require only paying attention.

On the archetypal level, my soul seems to gravitate naturally toward its own blossoming, as inevitably as crystals forming in solution. The me that God made is at root this beautiful, symmetrical, prismatic crystal. I wonder why the difficult journey is such a necessary part of it?

I have a favorite sweatshirt with a bristlecone pine on it. I love that tree. It grows older than any other living thing, nearly 5,000 years. It's used to calibrate archaeological dating, revealing the fluctuations in the C_{14} levels from year to year. The most fascinating thing about the bristlecone pine is that it only grows that old in locations where conditions are extremely harsh. It endures *because of* almost no rain, freezing winters, and blistering hot summers. It loves the craggy cliffs of the Southwestern canyons. Its siblings in more comfortable areas have a more normal tree lifespan.

Why should I be so drawn to the bristlecone when I've had a pretty comfortable life myself? Perhaps it's to squelch any tendency toward whining over my lot. Perhaps it reflects my love for the human bristlecones among us. I've always found them more of a treasure than the hothouse flowers among us. We are given a challenge in this life, not only of where we're going and what we're to do, but also of resolving the mess we're born into. Can the cruel blunderings of several generations of family end with me? Can I find a better way?

It's always seemed to me that I need to live out those blunderings myself before I can transform them. It would be so much easier to stand outside that whole mess and coolly decide to do better. And maybe some can do that. Unfortunately I've waded right in. I needed to be blasted by that departing lover. I needed to fall on my face. Those characters within can't stay unportrayed, unexplored. I can't understand Bill Sr.'s cavalier cruelty from the outside, and I have to recognize that cruelty in me when it's much more subtle than his.

No, the bristlecone tells me that it's the hardships I endure that make me hardy and enduring. Even now, in my illness, I suspect I'd fare better with less help. My grandmother wouldn't have had a choice; she'd have been harvesting and canning all this August, on top of beating the rugs and such. Perhaps that's just the therapy I need, within reason.

We are planning a peach canning session in a week or two. Perhaps I'm re-emerging into life after this solitary retreat. How I'd love to return to most of my life, with a few modifications—less vigorous activity, oxygen, naps. Can I reclaim the upstairs and return the study downstairs to its original use?

The current tests say my lungs are holding their own, not declining. That offers me a whole new outlook on life.

Wild Child

I was born into an unpopulated area, full of nature. Deep in the salt marshes of South Jersey, where the Delaware Bay narrows into the Delaware River, is a sweet little cove. The highest piece of land on that beach held a ramshackle hunting lodge, the Round House. At the turn of the Century it used to host wealthy Philadelphia hunters catching the spring and fall migrations of ducks and geese. More recently it held two elderly sisters. Dad wanted that place fiercely. He and Mother courted those sisters shamelessly with visits, pies, and jokes and finally did buy it from them for $400. Perhaps that was even a fair price for the thirties.

It sat a quarter-mile from the nearest road. Dad filled his trunk with oyster shells whenever he could and spread them onto the path through the meadow that got inundated with water. Electricity had passed us by, but kerosene lanterns worked fine, and I was proud of my most important chore of scrubbing their chimneys. There was no indoor plumbing. A hand pump was in the back yard. Our baths happened assembly line fashion, three round tubs across the kitchen floor. I was third to go through, so the two rinse tubs were pretty soapy by my turn. Mother allowed a fair amount of mess to keep it fun for us.

But the summertime more than made up for winters. We had a wide stretch of sandy beach with no drop off. At low tide we sat as toddlers in the shallow, warm water by the hour. It was many years before neighbors came and built summer cottages. Before that the beach was ours. I roamed it day after day, finding jetsom from passing ships and driftwood ready to sculpt. I knew to stand still so as not to disturb the magic of a muskrat swimming by. I learned two cries of the gulls, one that roused them to find the fish I'd apparently announced, and the other to bring interested males in search of the inviting female. They let me sit among them and watch their interactions.

We rarely had a boat, but for a while there was a little dinghy that I rowed deep into the meadow, following the narrow channels of clear water. I really wanted to get lost. That would be a worthy adventure. But I knew the landmarks too well.

My greatest challenge was once being overtaken by low tide while I was an hour into the meadow. As the water disappeared leaving very sloppy mud, I had to shift from rowing to paddling, and then to poling. Soon I was simply sitting on mud. I didn't think I could get out and pull the boat; I'd sink up to my armpits. There would be hours before the tide would lift me off again. Perhaps I could abandon the dinghy and make my way home across the mounds that grew bunches of reeds, though they were hard on bare feet and spaced far enough apart that I'd spend time up to my armpits anyway.

I honestly can't remember what I finally did. I loved those times fiercely. I could test my mettle. Mother believed in giving us a long leash. Be back by suppertime. Later she admitted to me she checked in on us frequently, but I didn't know that. I believed my life and safety were my own responsibility, and of course I should keep an eye on my baby sister until she could take over for herself. Mother had been given the run of a piece of woods as she was growing up and knew the importance of autonomy in nature.

What is that importance, especially now that it's so rare? I had direct access to God's world without another person inserting him/herself between me and it. No adult to take responsibility or interpret my experience to me, as in a summer camp. No well-crafted playground equipment that would simulate natural adventure. Certainly no video documentary to bring a vicarious adventure to my sheltered home.

I became a naturalist without ever thinking of science. I didn't learn the Latin names of anything, but I studied the design of many things, dismantled a few, and followed all of them through the seasons. And I became a contemplative without thinking of religion. When the breeze was cool, I'd lie in a dip of the warm sand and soak up warmth from above and below. The stillness made a falling grain of sand an audible event, as it shifted under me, slowly, quietly. My mind was mostly empty. I was a part of it all. One with the beach, the sun, the breeze, the gulls.

What of boredom, the bane of modern youth? We announced regularly to Mother how bored we were. Her solutions were often vague, like, "Go play outside." Often she set us up with creative projects: charcoal and newspaper opened out to the classifieds, or Ivory soap and a not-very-sharp paring knife. I remember early on playing office with Dad's discarded envelopes and paper. As soon as I learned to add, he gave me long columns of numbers to add up for him. Very soon this changed from play to a genuine service. I could hold the running total in my head and gallop down the page with increasing ease and speed.

It's interesting to me that all through school I was alienated from math and science. I belonged to arts and humanities. Clearly there's something amiss in the way we teach math and science, so divided and distant from our experiences.

Boredom is very useful. It's the gateway to discovery and adventure. It's the gap between turning off the mind's voice and the flowing of a deeper voice that comes out through our hands or our dreamy drifting fantasies. Both going outdoors and sketching on the classifieds invite the images of the deep unconscious to emerge. Beyond image even, it invites a oneness with the world that asks nothing of us, but washes over us as a blessing.

In these times we are not the center of the universe, we are a tiny piece, fitting in, in the same way as the muskrat, or the sand. From this vantage point we can glimpse that there is a God's point of view.

We were swept by passing hurricanes. They never did serious damage to us, and they provided excitement and danger. I always tried—often successfully—to avoid the first evacuation of women and children. I didn't want to run from the storm, but rather into it. One time I sat by the bulkhead and watched the rising water creep toward our lawn. It was dead low tide, nine feet below high, with maybe eight feet of extra water above that, and the tide was due to turn. Once the water topped the bulkhead, would it pull it down, and much of our front lawn with it? It came within inches of the top and hovered there. The passing winds were evidently no longer pushing seawater into the Bay, and then into this narrowing neck of land where the river begins. The suspense was gripping. I was discovered and sent to town, to my huge disappointment. Sleepless hours later I heard that the water was continuing to recede.

Another time, the winds whipped the river into a roiling cauldron. We had neighbors by then, and one had a raft anchored off shore. It was heaving and pitching in an irresistible way. I swam out to it, climbed on, and tried to hold on. I soon realized the danger involved. I took the spare rope and tied it tight across the raft, then slipped under it and held on. Half the time I was under water. I got into a rhythm of sucking in air as it heaved upwards and holding my breath as it plunged under. I became one with the storm in a furious ecstasy. The chaos and emotional turmoil of my adolescent life, as I longed for the adventures boys had and developed crushes on girls, were perfectly expressed by this wild ride.

Some of my adventures clearly went beyond what my folks condoned as an appropriately long leash. I must have been a trial. I don't think I'd do as well as they did if I were parenting me. I came away with keen senses. I can still smell and hear and see better than many. In college I could smell the traces of a friend who'd recently left the room I entered. I can spot the flicker of movement in the woods and hear the splash of spawning salmon in a distant stream.

I've never lost the ability to sit empty-minded, though I'm easily drawn into distractions as well as worthy endeavors. Being ill has encouraged times of floating in the here and now. It's not easy to see this as being equally important as, and maybe even more important than, accomplishing what I want to do before I die. My to-do list belongs to this world. My floating mind belongs to the world that's approaching.

Drama Momma

Drama has a bad reputation. We sit in our ordinary lives looking on drama queens, of either gender, with hooded eyes. When will they get over themselves? And yet, drama has been at the core of my life all the way through.

Early childhood make-believe is our way of enacting our fairy tales. We had virtually no media in my childhood, so our stories called for us to fill in a lot of detail and background in our own minds. Who did I enact? I remember pioneering themes—the Indian village, the beach explorer, and, of course, the Quaker garb that came out for special occasions. I can't remember creating variations on Cinderella, or even her prince. Perhaps they weren't our bedtime stories. And then Walt Disney came along with a version so overwhelming it was almost an invasion. My own imagination was left in stunned silence.

By our teen years we'd connected to the world and used drama to comment on it. With scorn, my sister Mary and I watched the men drool and assess the women in the Miss America pageant. We pinned up our hair that night, found fabric to pin down the back into slinky strapless gowns, painted our faces, and simpered for the camera in a pretty good imitation of Marilyn Monroe and Jane Russell.

When sack dresses became the rage, we fetched two feed sacks from a neighbor's farm and sewed them into dresses. They still smelled of the grain. I was afraid they wouldn't survive a wash. We climbed onto a bus and wore those scratchy things to some party I can't remember. I think we'd read in a magazine how ridiculously expensive the haute couture version was.

When I began to study French, I transformed the living room into a cliché cafe, with checkered tablecloths, candles in well-dripped wine bottles, and fake French signs on the walls. I'm still grateful for the cheerful willingness of everyone in the family to help out and play along. We must have borrowed heavily from the neighbors to come up with enough empty wine bottles since we had none. I expect it was grape juice we served up. Mary and Dad created a sultry Apache dance.

Mary was an eager cohort in all these exploits and Dad was a ham from way back. When I later found his high school yearbook, I saw he starred in two plays at least. No wonder we could talk him into these ventures so easily. He'd harrumph as if our ideas were ridiculous, but he'd never turn us down. Some of his Halloween performances became locally famous. I'm still sorry I missed the chicken he played one year I was away at school.

These times were real highlights. This kind of organic drama pulled us together. We were entertained not just by the end product, but by the entire creative process. We worked/played on the common endeavor. Without the endeavor, parents and siblings bicker and grate on each other. What can we talk about? Why can't we go do our own thing in peace, alone? These were our quilting bees and barn raisings, only more fun.

They gave me a vocabulary, a language for expressing my commentary not only on this beautiful and crazy world, but also on my inward life.

In the movies, James Dean burst on the scene with his perfect depictions of adolescent angst. In *East of Eden* when he moaned and rolled his head against the door jam, aching for his father's approval and his brother's girlfriend, an entire generation felt heard. And I fell in love, not so much with James Dean as with acting. I could do that. I could make the inner world visible.

In fact, it felt I was born for that. I couldn't hide my feelings to save my soul. Tears sprang to my eyes, I blushed at the slightest provocation; I might as well have signaled my passing thoughts and feelings with bright colors. I also had such a strong sense of empathy that I took on whatever physical symptoms a distressed friend had. My stomach would clutch up and tell me her whole state of mind. It often took a while, walking in solitude, say, to release her feelings and return to my own.

The Magic of Costume

I guess most people grow out of the make-believe stage of play. I never did. Because my early years were without electricity, entertainment was a homemade affair. I spent many solitary summer days as a cowboy in the wild West, an Indian in my Shredded Wheat village, a spy in Germany, a pioneer in uncharted territory, a wolf in the wild.

I was blessed with a family that loved to play. My mother loved her childhood rambles in the woods, and so she allowed us the same. I felt trusted to make sensible decisions, to not risk my life. The old school bell that called us to dinner could be heard all over the Cove. If we didn't show up for dinner, she'd worry.

Dad loved theater and costumes. Halloween was our favorite holiday. We had an attic that looked like a theatrical costume shop, thanks to Mother's packrat tendencies. There were Victorian bodices with leg-of-mutton sleeves, and suits with swallowtail coats—the real McCoy, inherited from grandparents, I guess. There was every Halloween costume ever used by us and several from others. The parts could be endlessly recombined.

When the road came in, bringing modern conveniences and neighbors, life changed dramatically. At first the neighbors were summer residents only. Our little neighborhood celebrated the coming and the going of summer with a parade. Someone would slip invitations under our doors, we'd rummage in the attic for costume parts and in the kitchen for makeshift band instruments. We'd meet at Otie's flagpole at dawn for reveille, a speech from the "Mayor" and the raising of the flag. Then we'd parade down the road as loudly as possible, looking for slugabeds. I remember marching right into Mr. Sowers's bedroom to wake him up—following behind his brother Otie's lead.

I can't think of a better way to cement a community together. Everyone got silly, the shell-shocked vet, the stiff wife, the kids and oldsters, the man with cerebral palsy. There's no way I'd be left outside that community. If I'd secluded myself, someone would have come after me, saying, I don't care who you are, you're one of us.

What is it that's so appealing about costuming oneself and taking on a different character? It is hugely satisfying, liberating. It's outside the narrow bounds we're allowed by society. We can make commentary on other people, the old, the young, the opposite sex, and by doing so, we comment on ourselves. To be stupid or high-brow stretches us into those things. The yokel's chortle we took on in costume pops out in other situations as a comment on our own yokel-hood, a short-cut admission or apology.

How narrow we are without these other characters. In fact, the many characters living inside me made the Easter bonnet and dress become tolerable. They were just another costume for another character. I look pretty grim in some of those Easter shots, but I can only imagine how grim I would have felt if that were the only character I was allowed.

Many Quakers in the Meeting had old Quaker garb tucked away in a drawer, to be pulled out for special occasions. I did my share of playing Quaker hostess for such events as the three-hundredth anniversary of the Meeting House. This costume had a special effect on me. With a dozen generations of Quakers in my blood, the bonnet and shawl sank me deep into my roots. I usually got teary and felt unworthy. I felt an obligation to settle my soul in quiet, to reach out and touch the souls of our visitors in ways I didn't understand. This was a different kind of character, not pushing the outer edges, but naming the center.

Elementary Zen — Lessons of a Dart Gun

I followed my sibs through the three one-room elementary schoolhouses of Salem's public schools. I remember the names of two of them as "Pig's Eye School" and "Cocked Hat School," though I can't get anyone else to confirm that. The one-room elementary school worked like this: the youngest first-graders sat in the left couple of rows, and got a lesson from the teacher on that blackboard. The teacher moved on to write problems for the second-graders on the middle blackboard. The right one got the problems for the third-graders in the right two rows. By the time the teacher got back to the first-graders the students were ready for her. This system worked all the way up through the eighth grade.

I usually did the problems as she wrote them on the board and then moved right on to the next grades with her. That made that year very interesting, but the next two years very boring, and one of the teachers, bless her, promoted me out of her schoolhouse after two years.

I was bored silly. I have no words to express the trial that this was. I remember once innocently carrying a letter home to mother from the teacher. Inside was a lesson I'd done in class, little sentences in perfect penmanship, only the periods were about a solid inch in diameter. The teacher's note was polite and puzzled. But wasn't that clearly an expression of my boredom? Class was so boring my brother Billy and I would race to the finish of the problem and its proof, always running our papers to her desk within a half minute of each other. I don't remember what we did while waiting for the others to finish. I do remember a lot of time was spent copying straight from the text to my notebook endless paragraphs about Mount Vesuvius or Lewis and Clark. Classroom discussions were not about these topics, they were about the teacher's grandson.

We had a substitute teacher in that first school who was a Quaker from Meeting. She called me "thee" and everyone else "you," much to my mortification. We'd used plain speech with Mother and each other at home and gradually dropped it for good as we went to school. Mother persisted in her one-sided use. Much later, in our 50s, my siblings and I realized we'd all but one returned to it in our individual families and when talking with Mother, and so we resumed it with each other.

Certain scenes have become family legend. Many of them involve Myrtle, the sixth, seventh, and eighth grade teacher, who taught my father when he was a boy, and who was beginning to lose it. She was famous for confiscating any rulers the boys twirled on their pencils—a favorite pastime for them and tempting to me too. Evidently, it was tempting to Myrtle as well. She twirled them down below desk level where she thought we couldn't see.

In Billy's class she confiscated a dart gun, with its darts, and wrestled with her conscience for quite a while. Now, Myrtle was as bored as we were. Worse. She'd pick one of the dumber boys to send to town for her cheese and crackers snack. Not our snack, hers. He'd come back a couple of hours later—town was three miles away. She'd count her money in little stacks of nickels, dimes, quarters while we worked on long division, sixteen digits divided by four digits, then multiply the answer to prove it right. These were long, peaceful breaks for her.

The story of the dart gun gets mythical, so I don't know how much of the legend really happened. Supposedly the principal of the whole school made a visit—an occurrence so rare as to be unheard of—and stood directly under two darts that were clinging tentatively to the ceiling by their suction cups, darts Myrtle had recently shot up there. He might even have watched one fall past his face. Myrtle just may have had to talk her way out of that one; it's hard to say with Bill telling the tale.

My poor sister Mary was so good she made "teacher's pet," much to her dismay. Her morning duty was to hook Myrtle's back garters to her stockings in the semi-privacy of the cloak room. Myrtle prepared for this task by turning her back and bending over. I made very sure nobody would mistake me for teacher's pet material. Hearing these stories, I anticipated Myrtle's schoolhouse with dread and glee, but nothing truly legendary happened during my tenure.

What saved me was the Encyclopedia Britannica at home. I was a true scholar in an area that believed an eighth grade education taught you everything you needed. High school was tolerated because it was mandated. I scoured the house and the local library for books. Luckily my parents had that old Encyclopedia Britannica, with few illustrations, small pages, and tiny type. It was printed on onionskin paper, which was so thin you were always seeing traces of the other side. Yet this set was my window on the world. Almost everything in these volumes was fascinating.

Re-tooling the Brain

I bided my time until I could go to George School, the Quaker boarding school our family attended. Bill, the oldest and the son, went for all four years. Mary, recovering from a siege of polio, went for three years, and I, the third, had two years as our family finances dwindled. My much younger sister, Jeanne didn't go at all, partly by her own choice. However it was a transformative experience for each of us who went. Somehow, we felt recognized for our unique, shining qualities. Somehow we were connected to the world and its problems in a personal way. We were inheriting this mess very soon, and it was possible to make a significant impact, to use our uniqueness to better things in our own way.

I entered a timid, half-wild child of the marshes. I was poorly prepared by the local high school for all of my classes. Third year French was conducted entirely in French. When I tried to protest, the formidable teacher interrupted me to say, "En Francais, s'il vous plaît!" She convinced me to stay in the class and to write down and look up any word I didn't know. Well, I was having trouble distinguishing where one word left off and the next began. But I struggled through that year until finally earning an A in the last grade period. What pride in that hard-earned victory.

The philosophy and religion teacher started the year with a huge assignment. He wanted us to write down our worldview and gave us an outline of questions to cover, all the great philosophical debates: What is time, and does it only move forward, the same for everyone? What are our dreams, where do they come from? Who/where were we before our birth, and what happens to us after death? What is God? On and on, for several pages. Once I started writing I couldn't stop. I had beliefs about all these things. I wrote 30 pages that night, all night.

He kept our papers for a long time, but when he gave them back they were covered with notes in the margin. He said things like, "Carl Jung says just this. Read chapter three in xxx." He connected us with the great thinkers who thought as we did. Our classroom discussions after that were bolstered by the big names. We didn't have to say, "I think..." we could say, "Carl Jung thinks..." I was astonished by the variety of worldviews in that room, and the respect for each one's legitimacy. I guess I'd thought that everyone thought as I did until then. What an incredible opening that was.

Let the Spirit Win

After finding the joy of being intellectually challenged I knew I wanted college. There was no money for it, and Dad's opinion was, "You don't need college to learn how to change diapers." I saw college as a shining doorway to my life's adventure. I didn't really care which college, and I knew it had to be inexpensive. I didn't even consider applying for a scholarship. I'd been bored and not challenged in Salem's public schools, but my two years at George School were sometimes a struggle. How smart was I? Were there SATs then? Was there any way to measure whether I was bright enough for the Quaker schools like Swarthmore, where I might have gotten financial help? I was far too timid and so much a loner I didn't have an advocate. I probably ignored the test days and scholarship days and recruitment days. Who did I think I was, anyway? Dad was always ready to tell me I was too big for my britches. There was simply no more money at home. I never visited any campuses. I gleaned impressions from a friend who did go visiting and settled on the cheapest, a little Protestant college in the South with strong arts programs. It served me fine. It focused my love of theater.

I got a reputation for arguing religion. In fact, New Testament was one of two courses I flunked, because I would not accept the professor's interpretations. I constantly argued the mystic's way, and the radical message of Jesus as a literal guide for our lives. When I raised my hand in class, he would groan, "Ah, another opinion from our resident Quaker!" I opened the final exam to find an essay question that asked for Biblical interpretation. I knew my choice was between mine and his, and I knew he wanted to see his. I didn't hesitate for long, and the choice to state my beliefs earned me my F. Later when I was applying for graduate studies in theater, the advisor asked me about it and then laughed heartily at the story. "Good for you!" she said.

This little college allowed me to breeze through most of my courses while following the directions of my heart. My freshman year the usual theater faculty of two went on sabbatical and were replaced by a gay couple who worked in professional theater as director and designer. They were rigorous and demanding, and inspired us to great heights. The community heard of the quality and came to plays from far away. In one year, actually in one play, I learned years' worth of acting training.

I played thirteen parts that year, many of them lead parts. Finally, I had an outlet for all the emotions within, all the characters. I felt breathed through, almost possessed by those people created by Tennessee Williams, Moliere and Chekhov. My grief and longing and petty jealousies were ennobled and opened to the assembled audience as part of the human condition, something we all know, whether we like it or not. I could feel my energy fill the house. I could feel the emotions in the audience. I could feel them hold their breath, begin to weep. I could feel them hate me and love me, recognize themselves in me. I learned how to link their emotions to mine at key moments, and play them like a musical instrument.

These two professors were a hard act to follow. When they left and the regular staff returned, several of us decided to take an alternate route. I didn't become a theater major. I began directing on campus with my talented friends writing and acting. The music department asked me to do the stage direction for their musical, *Brigadoon*, and in the next year, *Carousel*. I taught myself the skills, partly pretending to be my freshman director-mentor, but adjusting his techniques to discipline and direct my peers. I loved working with the whole visual image and the sweep of the story. I loved pulling those open-hearted moments out of others. I created my own theater major by acting and directing whenever I got the chance, and probably learned twice as much as the real thing.

There is something like the ritual of holy sacrament about the theater. We go to be opened, melted, fired up, left helpless with laughter. We go to be touched by the awesome power that is ever so much greater than the everyday. The actor's job is to usher this power forth, through her heart, through her naked honesty. There is really nothing else the actor has to work with but her/his honesty.

Of course, it takes a well-written script to express the truth in the first place. And each layer is a new layer of truth, added by the director, the actors, each of the designers. There is a large and complex team of artists creating set, costumes, lights and sound, all speaking the core genius that they see in the script in their own voices. It is a remarkable process.

Some productions I've seen—or created—had only one such magic moment, and yet that moment has pierced me and stayed with me ever since.

There were a lot of pre-ministerial students at that college, some as wickedly fun-loving as I was, but their course was to study the path others had taken. The Bible was an interesting series of accounts of the brush with the Divine, and of one who lived in the Presence. I saw our real job as writing our own Bible. How have we known that awesome Presence, and how did that change us? What a fascinating study that would be— live, first-hand accounts. If others had these experiences, outside of the kinds we had in the theater and music, they were hiding them. These taboo secrets were guarded closer than those of sex and money.

My Path, Which Way?

In college the student body had been divided between the "Bible Belt" and those of us who were creative, raucous, and irreverent (including some pre-ministerial students). That's where I took up smoking, unfortunately, in the renegade's lounge. I recognized that we all had a great deal of reverence, but our greater loyalty was to the truth, the wholeness of life. We poked fun at pomposity and dared to name and laugh at some of our own uniqueness, but we were not ready yet to name our loves for each other. It was the late '50s and very early '60s. I'd never heard the names for such feelings spoken.

My undergraduate degree was in foreign languages, mostly because I'd arrived with four years of Latin and three years of French. I started out as an art major and soon found that the assignments were more distracting than enlightening, more of a turn-off than a turn-on. I spent every moment of my freshman year at the theater but didn't want to major there either, especially with the sabbatical replacements, the gay couple who'd directed and designed in professional theater and had so influenced me, leaving and the regular folks returning.

I ended college dreading the return to South Jersey as an adult. That familiar populace had erased half of life, it seemed, the half that held a lot of appeal for me. My one persistent suitor, Jim, was stationed near San Francisco with the Air Force. Marrying him was my ticket west. California had a mythical reputation for beat poets, honkey tonk saloons and a town across the Golden Gate that had a Mayor who'd been a Madame. Normal life there was at least seasoned with a bit of wickedness. Deep down (and unacknowledged), I hoped to find others like me, even others who were drawn to the same sex.

Jim was not a Quaker. In California I laid down my outer Quakerism, but not the inward faithfulness. I was venturing into the deep woods of my own path and confronting the daemons there. I was listening to directives that I didn't think the Quakers would understand or approve of. And my deepest loyalty was not to them, but to my own truth, my wholeness. After all, in my experience of the Presence I was seen in my entirety, and loved for all of me. My path invited all of me, and I sensed that my usefulness at the end would need all of me. The Quakers I knew were tamed a great deal from that radical first generation. My loyalty was to that brilliant original vision. It seemed at that time I would have to travel alone.

Now I can look back and see how important my mother was to that fierce loyalty. She honored my true expression, even when it must have frightened her, even against my father's grumbling objections.

I arrived in California without job skills or clear direction. I spent several months as Jim's stay-at-home wife and soon exhausted the creative potential there. I was terrified of entering the job market with no experience and a useless resume. Jim and I both approached the theater scene by volunteering in the box office and business office. I eventually was a dresser backstage for a couple of plays. This was a far cry from directing musicals and producing plays I'd written myself, but the pounding of my heart made it clear that it was in the right direction.

Jim had seen me become Joan of Arc in Anouilh's *The Lark*, and he believed I had something to offer the theater world, bless him. I entered a Masters program in Theater and came alive. This was clearly on my path.

Years later, I was working in community theater in San Francisco and supporting myself with a day job that had me traveling around the wider Bay Area. One day I entered a brand new town created by a local developer, consisting of a housing development and a little strip mall. This inauspicious little strip mall housed an off-campus site of San Francisco State. I could hardly find the office. But strangely enough, my heart was beating heavily. This place was mine, I knew it.

In the office I got nothing but discouragement. They were looking for students and secretaries, not faculty. I went away, but I couldn't forget that school. I went back to San Francisco and found the urban pace too fast, the theater scene too stressful, my day job a dead-end street. I wanted to live in the country. I wanted to work in that little college.

As the Quakers say, "way opened" for that move. Once living there and gainfully employed in a bank, I broached the college again and still got discouragement. But I was ready to volunteer until they knew me better. It worked—I got a job in the theater department. I think it was meant to be.

A New York producer came to my play *The Dream,* which I wrote and directed at the college, and wanted me to take it first to Monterey/ Carmel where he had a summer home and then to New York for an off-Broadway production. It was "the big break" theater people dream of. My inner radar said no. Was that simply a terror of the big time? How much would this derail not only my plans, but also those of my cast? They weren't actors longing for the big time; they were majors in music, psychology, English, headed for their degree. How many of them would I have to recast and how would that impact the show, after all those months of deep dream work we'd all done together? Did this ritual of a play based on dream imagery lend itself to New York? It was with great trepidation and an aching heart that I decided not to go. The cast wouldn't go without me. I now can see how wrong that direction would have been for me.

If I've had a spiritual discipline, it hasn't been one of emptying my mind. It hasn't been one of service to humanity, or protest against injustice. That's why I've felt such a failure as a Quaker. I look back now and see that my discipline must have been to keep that connection with God alive and open, to express the inward messages in my art as well as in my life.

While waiting for my next direction in life, after teaching at the branch of San Francisco State that became Sonoma State, I spent a retreat with a member of the faculty of the Quaker Seminary in the Midwest. He was moved by my stories of experiencing the Light and invited me to apply for a faculty position at the school. I did, and when I got the description of what courses they needed a professor for I was dismayed. None of it fit me.

I've now been given the theological terms for this discrepancy. I was living "in the first moment" and the courses all were about "the second moment." I would have loved to offer what I knew of developing the mystical dialog, first moment stuff, but what they were looking for was Biblical exegesis, second moment stuff.

This has been my discipline. I used to talk about it as archetypal studies. I believe they are the same thing. My larger, deeper dreams have left me feeling brushed by the Divine. The purest expressions of my creative work feel brushed by the Divine. My scariest life decisions have been brushed by the Divine. Now, sitting at my computer with God's material splendor out my window, I see this world as brushed by the Divine. I can feel my Spirit more loosely attached to this body, and my presence in this blessed place a brief and priceless gift.

CHAPTER THREE

Bumblings of a Novice

Bumblings of a Novice
They're Learning — Get out of the Way

Teaching is clearly a calling. As I've practiced the discipline over the years, through several different kinds of venues, I've come to appreciate two sides to teaching. The first is the willingness to go back to what was once your cutting edge and craft the lessons there into a form that can hopefully create change and transformation for the student. This takes a light touch, the touch of a facilitator rather than a didact because the change is really initiated within the student. A teacher really leads a student to her/his inner teacher and then gets out of the way. And yet there is an art to the crafting of the lessons that accomplish that. And it does take a sacrifice of the teacher's time on her/his cutting edge. It's not easy to foster a student's output and produce output oneself. These are two different "cutting edges."

There's also a different side to teaching. This is inviting the unintentional lessons to happen. Here it's the teacher's job to be as transparent as possible. To allow students to see who you are and draw their own lessons from what they see. It's very important for the teacher not to try to actively "do" this form of teaching, for that leads directly to posturing an inflated ego around the room. Rather this is the opportunity for the Light to shine through—or not, as it will. You are sometimes a negative example—a terrifying thought. You are not the Buddha, you are quite simply real.

I wanted to aim them back to their inner source and not to stand between them and it. Don't we teachers love to take credit for what happens in the learning environment, after all we're the paid professionals. But I believe that the truth of what happens is not that teachers teach, but that students learn. The emphasis should be placed there. The "Great" teachers in my life have been the ones who asked me to lay my own material out on the table.

So I aspired to be the kind of teacher who directed students back to their own wisdom and helped them express it in the world.

Squelching

What happens when the free spirit inside is squelched? In my awake and thinking time last night, I was remembering graduate school and the thesis I proposed. I'd been reading the French playwrights from "between the two wars," as the French designate that early twentieth century time. I'd begun to feel the stories were all the same, the one noble standout refusing to go along with society's demands. I could see the spirit of the resistance and the fight for justice so many had joined in Spain. If you removed the outward style of writers as different as Claudel and Appolinaire, the message was remarkably uniform.

But my mentor and advisor would not accept it as my masters thesis because it was a doctoral level project, or, more accurately, the book I should write after my doctoral, when I would be ensconced in a tenure track faculty position. It was too big an idea for the masters degree. This was not the first time I'd been accused of having too big an idea. I ended up translating a book of theater aesthetics from the French. I hated almost every minute of it. There was nothing of my fiery spirit, my eager mind in it. It was plodding and safe. It should have been a French masters, not a theater masters.

Why do we do this? as teachers and parents, friends and mentors? It's not necessary to save people from their passions. Shouldn't these passions be listened to, drawn out, helped along as possible without taking over or influencing unduly? Aren't these passions that person's gift to the world, brought from the other side? When we say, "you can't do that because it's too big for you, you aren't old enough or well enough prepared," how do we know? We could be yanking Mozart from the piano.

The boy who dismantles every gadget he gets his hands on to see how it works, and the girl who drums on everything and asks for a trap set while still in grade school can be terribly hard on the parents, but what if we, as parents, watched for these areas of passion as the gifts they are, rather than annoying oddities. Wouldn't we end up with more brilliance in the world?

What happened in my mind when that thesis was squelched? Something deadened that remained dead ever after, I believe. My intellectual sense of adventure died down at that point, like clipped wings. I didn't go on to a PhD program to take it up again.

Disintegration

Fame will always elude me. I could never explore/exploit a niche endlessly like Andy Warhol until I was predictable enough to produce investment-level collectables.

In fact, it's in my nature to start over periodically. With Pluto on my ascendant I will be reduced to nothing every ten years or so. And it's been true that I go into a new profession, move and live with a new partner, have a major illness, etc., at about that interval. Do I get restless because I can't find the challenges in the old any more? It feels like I'm starting to repeat myself, and I can't stand that. It may have been that I never graduated from serial monogamy to long-term marriage in the career realm.

Being a teacher gave me summers off. Only once did I try teaching summer school, for extra money. It became quite clear that something very important was going on in my summer break. Sometimes I would lie in the hammock on the back porch and read my way through *War and Peace*. Pure input, after all those months of intense output. The seasoning on all this lay in watching the hummingbirds and the deer and the hatchlings in the nest over the door as they learned to fly. Long rambles with the dog, irrelevant projects like charting the last 30,000 years of human history. I always felt too complex to be a specialist. I always wanted the bigger picture.

So whatever specialty I invested in, there always came a time to lay it down, even when I didn't know what came next. Maybe especially when I didn't know what came next. "Surprise me" has always been a theme for me. The whole educational experiment a group of us developed at Sonoma State, Expressive Arts (a cluster school based on a community of artists-in-residence), was terminated for being too radical. And since we'd been required to take our tenure into the cluster school, we were effectively fired, even with tenure. Some elected for early retirement. Some stayed and fought, legally. I did neither. I figured that "way had closed" and God had another adventure for me. Actually I'd already gone to the division chair a year or two earlier and asked him if he had a list of volunteers should he have to lay faculty off. I wanted to add my name to the list. He was flabbergasted. There was no list, and why would I want to volunteer anyway?

I left the college when our cluster school folded and spent the next year or two simply earning money and asking for direction. I prayed to be useful. I offered up my hands to the divine purpose, and perhaps those years were used to great benefit that I don't easily see. I fostered a couple of extraordinary students through high school, one of whom is now a lesbian Episcopal priest, touching lives very deeply. Did I help that life path happen in some way? Perhaps.

What I really started out to talk about, though, was summers. Summers were a time for me of disintegration. I'd shun any goal-oriented activity. I'd search out emptiness. I'd drive to the desert and do nothing. Become a Gila monster. Watch shadows creep by and sand trickle in the breeze, much like my childhood summers on the beach.

One summer I headed out from my Sonoma County home to no destination with a friend in her old VW bus. We got as far as San Luis Obispo when the engine threw a rod, or seized up in some way I can't remember now. We called our friend Bob, who was a brilliant VW mechanic, and he came to us with a few spare parts and his tools. We unbolted the engine, stacked rocks under it, then pushed the bus out of the way and went to work on it. We dismantled it piece by piece, washed each little part in some dark, nasty liquid and laid them out on a towel. I think Bob took the head somewhere to get reamed out. Then we began to reassemble it meticulously under Bob's guidance. To our astonishment, it worked. We paid Bob—much too little—and drove off into the next leg of our adventure.

Now I can look back and see that as the very image for the work of my summers. Except that the new engine that was me was slightly different from the old engine—perhaps quite different.

There's a wonderful out-of-print book called *Operators and Things,* by Barbara O'Brien. In it, a woman goes through a schizophrenic episode while being aware of the process. She awakes to find creatures at the foot of her bed discussing her. They believe she needs a radical reorientation. They are the operators. She is the thing. They direct her to quit her job, say good-bye to her few friends, and drive westward. She disappears into a small town under their guidance, and holes up in her room through a period of "dry beach" mind. Occasionally a direction comes in on the waves and lands on the beach—often it is of a practical nature, like "buy some specific groceries." Meanwhile, the inside of her head is gutted and rebuilt with new mental structures. She's eventually given a direction to go to a specific address, which turns out to house a psychiatrist, who helps her through the last steps toward reentry into the world.

My summers were a shortened and less extreme version of that process. New mental structures. Individual parts cleaned and reassembled.

This period nearing my death is a summer-like task. I'm removing, examining, cleaning and reassembling the parts of my life. There is great joy in the task.

In my mother's last year she tried to sort through her crowded home to save us the burden. I watched her set up her favorite chair with a couple of full boxes from the attic on her left, an empty box and a trash can on her right. She gazed fondly at the pictures, even stroked them as she told me about them. She read through letters and notes, and even agendas from old women's club meetings. Everything went into the keep box; almost nothing went into the trash. I saw that she wasn't sorting, she was remembering. I realized that this was not about lightening the stuff in her house, but about pulling all the parts of her long life together, about valuing them, about loving those people and those times. She was finding the meaning in her having been on this dear Earth, what she had learned and what she'd contributed. It wasn't a time to throw parts away. She was loving the parts of her life and her old friends. She was trying to create a whole picture even though her memory couldn't hold onto the parts very long. I was moved to tears by the importance of this process. I told my siblings as well as I could what I'd seen and that we shouldn't push her to throw more away.

As it turned out, she moved in with my sister and we had an opportunity to sort through her things while she was alive without her watching and feeling the pain of our ruthlessness. We, after all, were doing a different process. We found many treasures and took them to her at the end of each day—a poem written by her mother, long-lost photographs, her high school yearbook, a stash of $20 bills she'd secreted away for the rainy day. She knew we were cleaning out the house, and she grew to trust us to do so carefully enough to not throw out the valuable things. I wonder if that lightened her load any. If that let her mind soften its grip on its structures and float free.

My dreams lately have been full of images of joyful floating free.

Keep Moving

Mary Oliver can say in a few words what I labor over for pages. She speaks for me. We worship at the same church, a church many of us are grappling to understand. Here's her statement on:

Praying

It doesn't have to be
the blue iris, it could be
weeds in a vacant lot, or a few
small stones; just
pay attention, then patch

a few words together and don't try
to make them elaborate, this isn't
a contest but the doorway

into thanks, and a silence in which
another voice may speak.

My friend Bill is a Conservative Friend, the kind of Quaker many people picture, reminiscent of the Amish. He has truly simplified his life—with homemade clothing and a tempo that matches the task—to a degree that makes me look like a hypocrite. I asked him once if he had a daily spiritual discipline. I was asking many people that question those days. He thought for a while, then said "I try to be grateful. Over time I'm remembering to stop and do that more frequently."

There have been times in my life when I've looked on my home and family, or my creative work and felt a profound contentment. This is beautiful. It is just what I wanted. Oh sure, there are things that need tweaking, and sometimes lots of work to maintain it, but this here before me now is just right. I am content, fulfilled. I could die now. That's how it comes out. I could die now.

Does that make it frightening? To be so satisfied I cease striving, which is to die? Does gratitude fall into that dangerous camp? What did I mean by that "I could die now"? That I'm in complete harmony with God's universe, and therefore in a way on the other side already—dead?

The French call orgasm *le petit mort*. It has exactly the same feeling of fullness, connection, and gratitude. We are designed to come to this complete a stop periodically. We maintain our health and happiness this way. This is an especially sobering thought for me when I consider how many years I went without a deep and shared orgasm. I believe those years were also more driven, with few resting points of pure fulfillment.

Perhaps in these times of "I could die now" I feel I've fulfilled my life's purpose, or what I've understood of it so far. If this is it, then these moments of gratitude, of stillness at the center, allow me to let go of that striving, that life purpose and begin to hear the next stage. Each period of my life ends with a little death.

The next period begins with all the bumbling of a novice. I have to start at the bottom again, often with a very humble job and dwelling. I have no skills, no self-confidence, no easy time of it. It's often in a new location where I'm not known and respected.

After a bout with Hodgkin's lymphoma I laid down the stress of a business restoring art objects and moved to Seattle to be with my new love, Margaret. It meant starting my life over once again. While I looked for suitable employment I cleaned house and ran errands for a "shut-in" who was not a whole lot more functional than I was. Margaret asked several times if I'd be the receptionist in her office, and I kept turning her down. It was too much togetherness. It was not my field: I didn't even type. It was, now that I examine my feelings more honestly, beneath me.

But this receptionist opportunity kept presenting itself. Each time I reconsidered it, it shifted to a slightly different undertaking. I began to see more and more ways I could be helpful with the talents and experiences I did have. I finally began to see the opportunity of this job as another time of starting anew as a beginner, on the bottom rung of the ladder. This awareness was the flicker that persisted. It was the flicker that patiently revealed to me that this situation needed me, and furthermore, I needed this situation. It took time.

Who am I at these times? Not a professor, not a successful entrepreneur. Clearly those things aren't the real me. Those accomplishments were not the ultimate purpose of my life. Something deeper is. Those accomplishments and accolades are answers. They are traps. If I stayed with them I'd stop moving. If I painted one great painting and then sat and admired it, how could I ever paint the next, very different painting? The old one has to get stashed in a closet. I know this is a very odd quirk. The norm is to find your own unique voice and then develop it for the rest of your life. For some reason I find myself scooping up the whole Rummy discard pile while others are busily emptying their hands. It may be a terrible mistake, a serious lack of discipline. Staying true to oneself is not always a clear path.

Enough, Enough Already

This morning I'm looking through old photos in preparation for some computer work, creating albums, or videos of my own life eventually, and my daughter Kindred's in the meantime. But I've awakened from a dream about vanity. In my dream, I am at the center of all my projects, and to what end? Who will care? Meanwhile I glimpse Christ (I think) slipping by almost unnoticed. Why am I drawing attention to me, when I should be directing people to him?

My perusal of old photos includes a whole album of photos from my theater work, along with programs and reviews. One of the reviews reveals the patchiness of the production, brilliant moments mixed with dull or awkward moments. Clearly I'm not a great director, though I made a big enough splash locally for it to go to my head. A great director would do whatever necessary to craft every moment to brilliance. A great director would sacrifice all else to this goal. A great director would have pursued the off-Broadway option. But if I'd chosen that I would probably not be able to work with actors' souls, to risk failure in uncharted territories, to value playful silliness. To work in a small campus was like working in my own studio, with the freedom to follow the flickers that need calm and quiet to be heard.

Ah, but greatness is such a brass ring. I've been seeking it all my life. How strange there's such an allure. Perhaps it's my emerging from the obscurity of the South Jersey swamps. The two primary messages I absorbed as a child about greatness were—from Dad, "Don't get too big for your britches," and from Mother, "There's always room at the top." No mention of that vast wasteland in between, where competition is fiercest and recognition slightest.

So what is good enough? What about local greatness? From my childhood, I well remember the local baseball team that our neighbor pitched for. We loved them and went to a lot of games. Those of us who played our sandlot games had a realistic goal of playing on that team. My sister danced in a local troupe that went on Ted Mack's TV show, The Amateur Hour. The next town up the road had a community theater that she and Dad acted for once I'd gone off to school. These days, our local skill level would be painfully lame compared to the standards of greatness broadcasting can bring us. We've become a passive audience of others' greatness rather than achievers of our own great-enough-ness.

Great enough is like all the other "enoughs" we're wrestling with at this juncture: enough gadgets in our homes, enough space in our houses, enough food and drink, enough work and stress, enough speed and power. Enough greatness to express what's unique yet universal within us, with enough skill to make the hair on others' arms stand up. That's what I want. And I also want to be able to relax afterwards with friends and go back to replacing the caulk around the sink.

Is it an oxymoron to speak of greatness for the many, rather than the few? Greatness for the few is a very patriarchal notion, where all life is ranged on some hierarchy, especially one based on how many people you have slaughtered and the closer to the top you are, the more worthy you are. The unfortunate corollary being that those close to the bottom are often dismissed as worthless. We are now struggling with the consequences of that kind of thinking.

Greatness for the many lets us all have our moments.

The Pilgrimage

I've come home from a two-week trip feeling profoundly moved. Moved first by how willing and helpful Margaret is in enabling this endeavor at all. She did all the driving, some with me napping in the back seat. She unpacked and packed the car numerous times, hauling the oxygen concentrator in and out of motels and up friends' steps. I'm humbled by how much assistance I require, and how cheerfully and lovingly she provides it. What would I do without her? That kind of dependency is terrifying. Am I really worthy of all this? Would I be half as willing and steadfast? I need to lay these worries aside and accept, graciously. I need to let her love in and feel the depth of it.

For several weeks before we left I finished sculpting several figures and edited video to be able to bring completed projects with me. I've always loved the idea of show-and-tell. And here we were staying with so many of my old friends who were artists and writers. Somehow, to read our writings to one another and to talk of the mysteries we were pursuing with our hands and minds deepened our time together immensely. I think we were aware that we might not get another opportunity to sit together like this and speak so deeply from the heart.

Each stop brought me back to a different part of my life, the time when they and I, or we, were sharing our lives more regularly. Now we were all aging together, wrestling with various disabilities and losses. And yet the work flows on, in all of us. I am enriched by their photography and theater, their sculptures and writings. There's just no stopping the flow of Spirit out into this world!

I played and handed out videos of that long-ago time when we were all in our prime, bursting with fun and energy. One was of the building of a house with woman labor—one knowledgeable builder and many other willing workers. What a testimony to what's possible, and to how generous people are with their time and strength, receiving in return a whole field of know-how and a lot of fun times. Another video was of several women clowns tap dancing through a grocery store and out into the woods.

They offered me, besides their current work, a batch of pictures from that time, new images of me and my daughter, one with my beloved movie camera. Gazing at the old photos, I see my young daughter Kindred echoing my posture and look, standing next to me while I'm directing from a script. I'm given back a new connection to that time. That time folds into me as a new layer, making me more whole.

Our destination was a reunion of faculty and students from the expressive arts school in Northern California. I loved hearing others' memories of events that I'd missed or forgotten. The intervening years had polished these moments into little gems, and all of us laughed and were enriched by them.

One man remembered a vain character from one of my plays who posed and strutted his way around the stage. The other characters onstage became a Greek chorus, saying, "Oooouuu! Ahhhh!" until eventually even the audience joined in when he came onstage. What a gift he gave me, to hand me back a lost image. We both laughed heartily. This effect echoed back to my college days when I'd seen Irene Pappas play *Antigone* in a Greek touring production. That chorus had raised the hair on my arms when they gasped or crouched all together, as much a single entity as a flock of birds. What had looked awkward in the reading of those ancient plays became the most powerful device present. I played with that effect afterwards in my own work, using it to externalize the feelings of a character or the audience, using it to spotlight a subtle moment or an offstage sound, or to lampoon our foibles.

My image for this trip is very modern. It comes from computer photo software, where one works on a complex picture in its distinct layers. One can put the layers together to see the effect, then separate them again to make adjustments to the individual components. On this pilgrimage I felt myself shifting and coming together into a single whole made up of these layers. Some layers are old and—I thought—well known, but I found myself making adjustments to my image of these times in my life as I saw these old friends more clearly. How much they've given me, more than I saw at the time. How much they still have to give me. How much I love them.

And how much they are giving the world, these old friends, and I with them. I can feel the movement we are part of, larger than any of us can see, and yet bound together, somehow singing the same song. Some working for justice, some for kindness or beauty, this tug we all feel is as strong and sure as the tug that pulls crocuses out of the snow in spring. I rejoice that I'm not alone. This dark time, so full of killing and corruption, is also birthing our song. God's song.

This whole panoply has become a picture of my life's song. It's been the same song all along, with variations and elaborations. And I felt the chorus we all made up, what a deep harmony we've made together, and still make, though separated by time and distance. That harmony stretches out to other kindred souls I don't even know. The key that keeps us together is our desire for faithfulness. Some respond to issues of injustice, others to inherent beauty. They are one song. They resonate together. How in the world can that be, if not for a larger picture than I can imagine? God's song is unfolding and has been all along. We've joined it to the degree we've been able to listen to, and beyond, the heart.

CHAPTER FOUR

When God Was Female

What Religion Is This?

Paleo Language

Then and Now

Squishy Earthy Stuff

Catching the Hand Axe

The Ancient Text of the God(dess)

When God Was Female

What Religion Is This?

I am trying to study another religion, one which has no living practitioners. The problems involved are many: first is how to remove the biases of this modern life, the second is how to interpret the clues left behind, the third is how to experience something similar in myself.

I read of an Australian aboriginal shaman drawing on a rock wall. His line disappears into a crevasse and later reemerges. He has gone on a spirit trip and emerged with new material. Those watching the shaman are asked who painted the drawing, and they answer "the Spirit." The shaman is insignificant except as a pure conveyer of Spirit.

A man lives with a tiny remnant of stone age people in Malaysia long enough to be trained as shaman—by being led deep into the rainforest over and over. No verbal instructions at all, which frustrates him no end. Finally his guide asks if he is thirsty (reading his mind?) and tells him he is able to smell water. He realizes he can and succeeds in finding a leaf full of collected rainwater. His guide slips away and leaves him to his own devices, which first panics him, then opens him to the forest as never before, and to the mind of his nearby guide, and to an awareness of the distant village, and to a tiger who accompanies him home from a distance. He breaks through to a Paleolithic mind, which is at one with the rainforest. Some of us have experienced moments of this oneness. It is our heritage.

Yet even though it is our heritage, we are locked into belief systems that prevent us from experiencing much beyond these few glimpses. We believe we are above other animals, let alone plants, rocks, streams and winds. In fact we believe they exist for our benefit for the most part. Most of us know animals only as pets, where their animalness is kept infantile and subservient. Language is the province of humans.

I once spent a day ripping vines out of a Live oak tree in my little patch of woods. As I worked, I became more and more dismayed at the extent of the intrusion, which I'd been only dimly aware of. I cut free a large mass of vines and pulled them out of the crown of the tree, trying not to damage too many leaves and small branches. I mentally apologized for the damage and in response was flooded with aroma, and the sense that the tree was telling me the damage was nothing compared with the freedom it now felt. Gratitude! The sweet tang of Live oak was an overwhelming gift of gratitude. Tears leaped to my eyes. Ever after that tree was special to me. I talked to it whenever I passed. Such a tiny fragment of Paleolithic mind that I can hardly imagine if all my daily life were so lived.

Another time while bare-bones camping I sat by a stream for most of an afternoon, not reordering my life back in the world, but simply appreciating the peace and beauty, letting everything come to a halt. I let my hand hang in the water, which was still and shallow, crystal clear with clean stones below. A curious fish swam up and paused just below my hand. My sense of peace enveloped the fish. I casually stroked it from head to tail, once. It received the entire stroke and even a moment more before darting off.

Many years ago a wonderful film came out about the Tasaday of Mindanao, another remnant of stone age people, almost untouched by the modern world. In one scene, several adults sat in a circle talking. Every once in a while the speech would lift into a little flight of unstructured song, not so very different from our own speech when we're bursting with wonder and excitement. I got chills. I felt I was seeing the origins of song. After the little interval of heightened expressiveness, the voice dropped back into speech again. The others smiled and murmured, laughed quietly in appreciation.

The indigenous people of the world have so much to teach us—if it's still possible to learn. We watch their cultures become extinct at a very rapid rate. The bush people of the Kalahari have lost or are losing their habitat, and therefore their forager way of life. We must, and I believe we will, come to appreciate the importance of these ancestral ways of life, but it may not be in time to save them.

Indigenous people and their knowledge are important because that was our way of life for millions of years, enough time to evolve around those realities, those needs. How you eat for a million years determines how your gut works. How much time you spend basking in the afternoon sun for a million years becomes an important clue to our own stress reduction and peace of mind.

So anthropology is leading me toward an understanding of radically different, and yet familiar, ways of interacting with the world. It helps me interpret the archaeological sites and artifacts as well, sometimes at variance with the standard interpretations. My attention is focused on the artifacts, the art, of these people, and especially the art that depicts humans rather than animals.

Paleo Language

I've been pondering how the creative explosion of the Upper Paleolithic came about. Many say the answer is language, as if that were a single development. I suppose they picture us grunting one decade and chatting the next. Language is such a huge field that the question really is what stage of language could have made this huge a difference. I'm sure we were talking freely to each other within our little village communities, but how did we make the leap to a lingua franca?

My granddaughter has just left from a visit. She's almost two and has no words yet. She speaks in rolling phrases that reflect her opinion of our speech as essentially music to accompany the gestural communication of meaning. She participates thoroughly in our collective song, delighting in its patterns and rhythms. Some of her utterances capture the sounds well enough to be a clear "there you go" but most roll along like a babbling brook. She is clear as a bell about what she has to say, though, most of the time. She picks up my oxygen hose to ask me to go with her because she sees me carry it. She pats the floor next to her to ask me to settle in for a while. Her gestures are accompanied by a lilting flow of sounds that echo our speech. Sometimes it's the intonation that gives us her meaning. She is pre-English, but not really pre-speech, and certainly not pre-communication.

There is another aspect to language, and that is how it is used—in what service. I'm reminded of the story of the bonobos who came across another tribe. First the males rushed forward and performed their frightening performance of screeching, jumping and waving sticks. They then retreated behind the females, who moved toward the female strangers, kids tagging along. The females greeted each other, finally settling in to groom and even make love to each other. The kids played together. The males saw that things were okay and joined the others.

It may well be that we are hard-wired with the same instincts and social jobs. Men meet any new or threatening situation with strength and equal threat, ready to protect the rest. But women are curious to exchange news and build bridges. Fight-or-flight versus tend-and-befriend. Perhaps the Upper Paleolithic began when women came into power and structured society more on their model.

I dreamed last night of a Miss Trenchbull-type of matron (a character from Roald Dahl's *Matilda*, best described as a bitter tyrant of a headmistress), who arrived for my granddaughter Genevieve, either as stepmother or preschool teacher. She said something about her being the one she was to take control of. I (horrified) corrected her to *take CARE of.* I wonder if that is the heart of the difference between the male way and the female way. And, as evidenced by our nation's extreme imbalance, the less you care for, the more you have to control, as people rise up to get their due, to try to change things, to even survive.

This is the wiki era, when information is available, free, supplied not by a few "authorities" but by everyone contributing their piece of expertise. This revolution echoes very closely the Upper Paleolithic revolution. Our communication has taken another leap, actually a quantum leap, forward.

Paleolithic people built an amazing community that spanned the Eurasian continent, as shown by the amazing similarity of their artistic expression. The palm-sized female figures share many conventions, the bowed head, hands on breasts, nakedness, facelessness, a neglect of the extremities and focus on the torso, and yet they are full of individual expression and variation. They come in all ages and weights, in several materials, with more probably made in perishable materials. The sculptors had a topic they were all talking about, and they added their own observations, their own voice to the conversation. If they were a jazz band, they'd be adding their unique instrument to the same tune. Of course, they talked about a lot more than the Divine Feminine. They shared freely every good idea they had. Fish hooks, needles, atlatls, specialized blades, and tiny tools for boring.

Their lack of clutching paranoia shows how lightning fast and liberating the sharing of information and goods and the meeting of needs can become when we are not trying to control from above. The academic control of information is, among other things, to guarantee its accuracy, but, when examined, it guarantees only the exclusion of other points of view. Men's control over women is to guarantee the paternity of their children, and that appears to have been an impossible goal, even with chastity belts. As for the goal of silencing women's wisdom? Even with the "Scold's bridle" (a device comprising a metal face mask with an attached spike that went into the mouth, which was used on housewives from Inquisition times until the early nineteenth century), that was impossible.

The wars the United States and other military powers wage are to control our systems of exploitation of natural resources and human labor around the world, and all of this is proving untenable. What a relief it will be to finally let go of these draconian measures of control and get about the business of building the worldwide community.

Then and Now

This morning I dreamed of taking Margaret back to my old one-room schoolhouse, to my beginnings. There was a banner of threads with names attached to it. I knew, as if I could see a film of it, that I had attached my name at the very beginning. We walked down the row of names until there it was, LYNN, the first name on the banner. I was flooded with the sense of completion, having linked the present me to the me that began it all. We were the same. There was a completed loop. It was all one journey, one person, one destiny.

I suppose people who live a more connected and coherent life don't feel surprise at a revelation like this. It makes me wonder if my radical shifts of profession weren't a way to try to dump the past and start over again. A whole new me. As if that were possible. Or desirable.

There's a great value in looking back at the original sketch as it were, the prototype of who we are. Many years ago, I sat with my friend Barbara looking at the photographs of my childhood. She pointed out how clear and present my eyes were in the earliest shots, and how they progressively clouded over, grew more wary and cautious over the years.

It's taken years to scrub away the protective barriers and let my original self shine forth again. We don't even know who we are—who we can be—through many of those years, in my case stretching through the prime of my life. I suppose it echoes the picture I imagine of our coming into the world a pure soul, as God made us, and then not recovering that state again until that glorious moment of seeing the Light at the time of our death.

This time of creative outpouring is so rich for me. The three broad areas: writing this, sculpting Stone Age women, and editing video all crowd around waiting their turn to come out. It feels as if they are three broad-shouldered men trying to pass through a doorway at the same time, getting jammed sometimes, politely jockeying for order at other times. Yet they're not really three separate things. They keep visiting each other and adding new insights.

When I work with these sculptures, I am brought back to my beginnings, almost clear enough to see the LYNN stitched in their banner. This is another loop that for me connects the early Paleolithic prototype with what we are all trying to create in our society now. That was apparently a time when peacefulness and justice were taken for granted, easily achieved, as incredible as that may seem to us today.

Many are skeptical and call such opinions sentimentality and mere wishful thinking. Yet what we've found in one archaeological site after another are signs of equality and caring for one another. There are no grandiose palaces or cathedrals, and no slums, hovels or jail cells. There's no sign of armies or defensive fortifications. There are no signs of a social structure where the one forces obedience of the many through mutilation and murder.

Why should we find that incredible? Shouldn't it be the other way around? Isn't it incredible the degree to which we've accepted such atrocities as normal and allow them to happen? There is a natural instinct against killing one's own kind. Throughout the animal kingdom threatening behavior toward one's own kind is designed to intimidate and discourage, and then to stop short of harm. Shouldn't we be asking when and how in the world that ever broke down in human prehistory?

When looking at the times when women were so prominent, we must look with unbiased eyes. It's not a feminist bias we need to guard against, as is usually meant, but the "killer ape," patriarchal bias. What the clues suggest is astounding.

I disagree with Rianne Eisler's popular and now widely accepted characterization of Paleo- and Neolithic times as a "partnership society." What I see is a matriarchal society, one in which there is no evidence of war, where all people's needs were met and where the female was clearly revered. Yes, the notion of power does need to be redefined, and not simply by flipping patriarchal power on its head.

There is a distinction between sacred and profane sculpture. The sacred carries certain clear conventions such as the taboo against portraying the face, and the exaggeration of the female attributes to the extent of omitting irrelevancies like feet and arms. Among the sacred sculptures there are few male figures. Among the profane are several that help us get a picture of everyday life and typical male activities. Interestingly enough, the men are not depicted killing either animals or other men. They are playing the harp, conducting a religious service (perhaps) dressed in an animal skin, and dancing with a bull. Their life was as radically different from now as the women's.

In spite of these important clues, men's lives remain a relative mystery. The women dominate the scene so thoroughly that it seems clear to me they defined the society. It was a women's time. The partnership society that Eisler sees back then belongs to our near future. It is what we long for with all our hearts, and is what we are trying to bring into being. That is our task at hand. But I don't think we can look for a model to copy from back then.

What is important is to see the women's world and learn from it, for men to do this without trying to jump in and claim it for themselves. To put together both halves now, we need to see both halves clearly.

Squishy Earthy Stuff

I'm drawn to sculpting in clay. What is it about this squishy, earthy stuff that is so appealing? Sliding my thumb along a curve to shift just this much material from here to there, to feel it slide with me and cling to itself at the same time. It is very willing to mold itself to my wishes, and it lets me know it has its own demands, it belongs to its own muddy roots. It's a dialog between something deep in here and something deep out there.

The mind rests. Sculpting has nothing to do with the mind. It can watch, bemused, or just go on holiday. This is the older wisdom of the hands. They can find and express an image that I had no idea was important to me until it's emerging.

I've been captivated by the prehistoric depictions of the Divine, because, at that time, the awesome was seen as female. For the last fifty years I've been reading about them and staring at their pictures. For the last twenty I've been surreptitiously collecting reproductions. I don't really *approve* of collecting ceramic knick-knacks, and here I was with several Paleolithic fat women tucked into my bookshelf.

And yet gazing at these reproductions freed me from the tyranny of others' interpretations. I'd already learned to study the pictures and raise my private little cry of protest when the old school male archaeologists drew their clueless conclusions. These sculptures gave me a three-dimensional picture; I could see their backsides too. I began reading closer to the source. Where were they found, and what kind of a community was it? What else was found there? The text would show four animals and one woman when the dig really had four animals and thirty women.

The societies I saw emerging were marked by equality, what appeared to be peaceful, cooperative justice. There was no sign of war, economic extremes of power or poverty, even in the large Neolithic cities. It was very exciting to see a society so like what I long for now. There was a sense of connecting back to some basic truth. This madness of money, war, and power that we live in was not natural. We're not red in tooth and claw. We know how to do it right, and spent tens of thousands of years doing it right. There is hope.

At the center of these peaceful cultures lie the statues of women. They span almost the entire Stone Age. I'm awed by their exquisite artistry. There are so many abstractions of the female form. It is an endless symphony of praise. They express a full range of power and dignity, grace and authority. They restore my soul. They remind me that woman is awesome. For perhaps the first time in my life, I feel I am made in God's image.

When Margaret and I built our new house, I designed a gallery for these statues in the living room, open shelving that made a divider for the entryway. I was surprised at the number of figures I had. What arose was a recognition that the *collection* was the emerging work of art, rather than the individual figures.

I looked at my handwritten cardboard labels and longed for better. Research into dates, sizes, and materials went into a layout on my computer that got printed onto metal and cut. My woodworking friend made me walnut easels, and suddenly it looked like a museum.

I noticed some of the bases were pretty funky—a bent coat hanger glued into wooden craft store plaques. I'd been prowling thrift stores for tchotchkes with usable marble bases, but most of these looked too civilized for the Paleolithic era. So I prowled a rock and tile remnant yard and found a treasure trove of natural rock in small chunks. I mounted the Neolithic on cut and polished stone and left the Paleolithic bases rough-hewn. I was really getting carried away here, but so far nobody was challenging me.

All along I'd felt a hungering for sculptures that weren't available for purchase, not so famous, yet stunningly expressive. I tried to interest my daughter and my niece, both sculptors, in making reproductions, but neither wanted to take this on. It took a while for me to get it that this calling was for me. I had no idea how important this task would become.

I bought ten pounds of clay, a very cheap investment. I scanned and downloaded pictures of every angle I could find of each original, got its measurements, and printed pictures in its exact size. Not much risk. I could always throw it away and start over. I had done some sculpting, so I wasn't an absolute novice.

What ensued was a wrestling match between that figure and me, still full of my modern attitudes and experience. My first rough-in was a caricature, larger than life and full of my commentary. Yet it looked perfect to me right then. The next day I could see the most obvious problems and correct them. For several days running I gradually tamed my own enthusiastic message and listened more closely to that alien message from so long ago. My task was to express it as if it had been my own all along. That message seemed utterly new, while at the same time feeling utterly familiar.

Many years ago, I dreamed there was a primitive hand axe hurtling toward me across the intervening ages and cultures, crunching its way through time. Someone had hurled it to me, but it was a little off course, destined to pass me by. I hastened to step into its path. Was I planning to catch it? To let it penetrate my chest? I have no idea, but I knew it was for me, and of great importance. Was the dream telling me to pursue this interest, so long ago? Was it this gallery calling to me? It is not finished yet. I've added eight reproductions that I've sculpted and six more are in the works, not yet fired.

What did those monks experience who spent their lives copying illuminated manuscripts? They must have known those scriptures more thoroughly than anyone, having taken them in and printed them out word by word, letter by letter, singing the cadences, awed by the brush of the Divine. And to top it all off, they painted scenes to capture the feel and magic of the message. They knew they were saving something that would otherwise be lost to their own time and all times after.

These sculptures have been lost to us, except in books. They are scattered in museums large and small all over Europe. The larger museums carry a collection of reproductions, but where in America, where in the Northwest, would I go to see all these together? Yet these sculptures are just what we need, or at least they are just what *I* need. But why? Perhaps to really answer that I need to sculpt them, to take them in, curve by curve, and put them out, faithfully, like the monks.

During this process the modern world slips away. These figures come from a time when truths were expressed not in books full of words, but in a single image, mysterious enough to contain echoes and harmonies of meaning. Until recently, their time was called pre-history, and it was adamantly proclaimed that nothing could be known of this obscure time. Fortunately, archaeology has grown up from its treasure-hunter beginnings into a sophisticated and complex science that is telling us volumes about how people lived. But there is a limit to how much science can help us understand these evocative women.

For this we need to rely on those scientifically suspect realms of art appreciation, dream interpretation, and religious symbolism. Just as in approaching biblical stories, the questions of where, when, and even if are not the avenues toward meaning. It takes asking *why* to open them up. Even if the history is thoroughly debunked, the question remains: Why is this story told and retold; why does it unfold this way?

Just so, the questions of whether these women are goddesses can be debated into the next millennium. They are here, looking peculiarly themselves, full of quirks. To accept the quirks just as they are, to be amused and delighted, puzzled and disturbed—this is the path toward understanding.

Catching the Hand Axe

I was pulled back into sculpting by Hamangia (named for her culture, in Romania), a figure dating to 5000 BCE. She seems clearly a divinity, where with many sculpted figures this is not clear. Numerous sculptures are in her style: long, tubular neck with no head, etc. There is also a pair of figures who are clearly not divine. They sit casually; they have faces; they are wonderful subjects from the village for a sculptor to take on. The contrast between these and the Hamangia-types is exciting, and clear as the tone of a bell. As a modern sculptor, I find these two casual folk much more interesting subjects.

But as a student of the Divine, I've turned my focus onto this woman of great dignity. She is full of ancient conventions. Her legs and neck have an edge on the front and back, like well-pressed pants, with a triangular pleat where the groin and knees would crimp them. These and other conventions mark this culture. They mark Her as theirs. She also carries conventions that go back 20,000 years: her prominent pubic triangle, her hands under her breasts. Looking forward, after her, one can see the roots of the Cycladic nudes, with their formal, straight stance.

As I sculpt it amazes me how critical it is to get her legs just right, not too fat to be graceful, not too thin to be strong. Her belly tucks in to make a crease just above that huge pubic triangle. Her arms wrap around under her breasts and meet in the middle, evoking a circle around each breast. And doesn't this torso look like a face with eyes and mouth! These are my meditations, miles away from words and concepts.

What is it that enters me during these meditations? Something flows in, through my eyes, through my hands. My focus, my vigilance is a faithfulness, a staying true. To what? *To that hand axe.* It chose me, way back then, and I accepted by stepping into its path. We're going way beyond Quaker faithfulness, Christian faithfulness, or modern ecumenical faithfulness here. I'm being led into the deepest jungles of Borneo. Nothing of what I know so well is of any use to me now.

For God is female here. That much is clear as spring rain, in spite of the equivocating the professionals want to do around that question. When I started out, that wasn't so profound or disturbing. The Goddess is a shopworn cliché by now. Some characterize Her as a fertility goddess, or some other attribute that belongs to a primitive long ago and far away. Some women want to make Her immediate by proclaiming that we are all goddesses.

First of all, the word goddess makes me look around for the god who must be her other half. The word God covers everything. She was nobody's other half back then. She was God. Really, if you're looking for a human image of the awesome, women fit very well, having the ability to bleed without dying, gestate and bring forth the next generation, and then feed the young and vulnerable from their own body.

From the clues, she was central to the tracing of ancestry, the creation and maintenance of community, the gathering and preparing of food, the weaving of clothing and shelter, the administration of fair sharing and justice, and the major inventions connected with all these things. She was awesome. And so are we, only it's a very well-kept secret.

My generation of girls was raised to never seem smarter, stronger, or more mature than our boyfriends, and later husbands. Our job was to make him look good, so he could go through the world with all the attributes of both of us, our figurehead, who got all the credit. We played the same role as executive secretaries, research assistants, and speechwriters. We were to remain conveniently invisible. Even to ourselves. We gave away awesome.

And now I find I can't recognize a voice in a dream as coming from God because it's a woman's voice. My head can say God is not male, but deeper down I have to admit I'm still protesting (God is male! But wait, no He isn't). This one is deeply ingrained.

Sitting here pushing the clay with my thumb from deeper in the dip to higher on the hump, feeling the drag of earth and the willingness of mud, I realize I'm tracing the moves of that other sculptor 7,000 years earlier, feeling my way toward truthfulness, participating in the mystery by bringing Her forth. She lives in me as She did in that sculptor. God is not time-bound.

The Ancient Text of the God(dess)

A new rush of ancient figures has come tumbling out of me, just when I thought I was done. I looked back through several of my books and noted the new ones that spoke to me. One such is the lower half of a woman with a nest, or bowl, scooped into the top, where her waist was. In the nest are two eggs, sitting approximately where her uterus is. She has what appear to be eggs drawn on her thighs and buttocks.

I missed this one before. The pictures are very small, and drawn schematics only. They came from behind the Iron Curtain at a time when funds for archaeology were scarce. Seeing it clearly was like finding a tiny treasure in a dusty corner of the house. What an astonishing statement from a Neolithic village.

I printed the three angles at the size of the original piece, plus shrinkage allowance. And then my hands took over. Art is such a satisfying merger of craft and heart and mind. It is so satisfying to finish an intellectual pursuit with this tactile, physical statement. There are so many unanswered questions here. Eggs I can relate to; the intriguing part here was *pairs* of eggs. Were twins seen as a special Divine blessing? Were these linked to the pairs of women, the "double Goddess" that appears throughout this time?

With my hands working the clay, I didn't have to find answers; I could simply take in what is. This in itself is not a small task. There is a similarity here to listening to someone without formulating a response or a next question at the same time. Just listen. Just look.

My secret opinions creep out into the clay. I see a caricature appearing before me, filled with my own commentary. Luckily I have those life-size drawings to keep bringing me back. I discover her delicacy and grace. I notice that her big hips and tiny feet make a heart shape. Her belly shows the early stages of pregnancy. Her skin is covered with symbolic writing.

She is an ancient text. These are the manuscripts of the Neolithic. They are not filled with words, as later texts are, but rather with images. Just my cup of tea! They are likely filled with story and myth, philosophical musings and reports of contact with the Divine. They feel as rich as the book of Isaiah.

Clearly the awesome, central mystery of life and life's cycles is portrayed as female. God is female. That in itself is profound for me, after so many years of Lord and Father, with all His prophets and priests, an entire world that doesn't include me. I was not made in the image of God, evidently. God might be *in* me, but was He *of* me? We know how painful it is to be left out of games on the playground. How much more painful to be left out of the life of the Spirit. To see no reflection of oneself in the Divine. It's a wonder to me that all women don't throw over their religious traditions in disgust.

I was sheltered from some of that by our nature-based life and the Quaker spiritual practice that honored women so highly. There was very little Bible in our Christianity, and what there was, was a careful selection of the loving and inclusive parts. Even with that, there's no escaping the wider culture.

Here in these lumps of clay was proof that I am indeed made in the image of God. And that the true mysteries are of nature's self-perpetuating bounty. Ask for an egg, and you might get two.

This Gathering of the Goddesses that is happening in my living room has taken on a life of its own. The sculptures on these shelves are a whole history of the missing images of the Divine. Their scope is magnificent. They are an embarrassment of riches, like a huge collection of dreams that can be explored endlessly for meaning. At times I feel I live in a temple and have dedicated my life to keeping Her alive and well in the world.

My mother-in-law asked what would happen to these Stone Age female figures after I die, with a faintly audible hint that they ought to go somewhere public. What an interesting thought. Perhaps they should. But at this point I'm just listening for directions. With six new pieces drying for the kiln, and a piece of alabaster waiting for the knife, those directions clearly haven't stopped coming.

Mercurial Freedom

Mercurial Freedom

Image

I discovered the power of image in the early '60s, through my association with the Jungians in San Francisco. I went into therapy there and learned the rich language of my dreams. I first had to learn the discipline of capturing those images, with pen and paper ready by my pillow, faithfully recording every offering. I then learned that their language was my own; I couldn't refer to a symbolism dictionary. I had to let them work within me as their images grew clearer and more powerful. The therapist encouraged me to draw as well as record in words, to be precise, to find the heart of the message by looking for where the emotion bursts through.

Through this process I began to honor the images and their mysterious source more and more. They could nail me to the wall with absolute accuracy. They knew me far better than "I" did. They brought me new material, new insights, new truth I often didn't want to see. But the naming of those truths left me feeling more balanced, more relaxed, more at ease with myself.

I began to make periodic summaries in my dream journal. I'd reduce the dream to a sentence or two and list the dreams, one after the other, on a page. What I found was that they had an additional meaning beyond their individual statements, a meaning in their running narrative. One striking example began with a dream I had that I would die for two weeks. I prepared two coffins for myself with open, screened windows. For the next two weeks my dreams were "from the other side." In one I told someone of this odd dream I'd had, and on awakening, found that that image was clearly from my daily life of approaching death here!

Exactly two weeks after the coffins, I dreamed of returning home to tour the neglect that was evident in my grocery store. There were unstocked shelves and even human babies being sold in the meat department. Who's minding the store? It was time for me to take charge again. The underneath narrative was strong, the images that expressed it very fluid. They could change reality whenever they wanted, whenever the new reality said it better. If I could let go of the surface reality that I usually grip so tightly, then I could see the images as metaphors in a sentence made up of a series of dreams. My task was to construct sentences out of these dreams and a story out of the sentences.

There was another necessary process. I strongly felt that the images had a range of importance. In Jungian terms, some were openings onto the archetype, carrying an incredible force. They haunted me whether I understood them or not. Others seemed lighter-weight, some almost throwaway. I saw those as a more personal commentary on my daily life. It was crucial that I test whether those images with power for me also had power for others.

With theater as my medium, it was natural to see the story as a play rather than a written piece. I began collecting dreams that had a strong story line and theme. The more I worked with them, the more they—almost on their own—merged into and transformed each other, without losing the bizarre imagery that had compelled me to include them in the first place. An example from the first act of my play, *The Dream*, conceived and performed at Sonoma State:

> *Early in the play, the dreamer leaves her own farewell party to fetch her mother, who has promised her a ride to the train station. But her mother is weeping, devastated on her bed upstairs, "in no shape to drive her anywhere." Disappointed and angry, the dreamer leaves, but is captivated by a little, high door on the stairwell that pops open. She reaches up to close it, but it drops off in her hand. She brushes at the cobwebs inside. Her mother leaps out of bed and opens her door. Her "Don't touch that!" makes the dreamer flinch.*

> *The mother, step by step, moves from her fierce command into a verbal seduction. "There's nothing there you'd be interested in ... If you have extra time, come visit with me ..." She removes her robe and lets down her frizzy hair. The dreamer is mesmerized by the*

combination of warmth, hidden power, and sleaze. She returns to her mother and lets herself be drawn down onto the bed. The mother pins her down and leans to kiss her on the mouth. The dreamer finally snaps out of her trance enough to struggle. The mother holds her down, all elbows and knees, like a spider, still drawing her in with her voice.

The dreamer drags and claws free, crawling across the floor to the door. She reels and staggers down the stairs as her mother wails her loss. She lands in a heap at the foot of the stairs, at the feet of an ancient crone. The crone finally asks her, "Are you ready to leave now?" The dreamer pulls herself together to follow the crone through her next adventure.

I wanted to stay true to dream structure, where the images have a mercurial freedom while the underlying process moves ahead relentlessly, and hopefully clearly. I envisioned scenes emerging out of the crowd of audience and cast together, and, when done, melting back into the crowd. I saw the audience seated on pillows throughout a room that had small, low stages scattered throughout. Actors looked like audience until they stood and stepped onto a stage. The main character, the dreamer was the one driving force moving through these scenes.

I started work on the project by offering an acting class to explore the play. I cast students in a single role and asked them to explore the role and the scene as if it were their own dream. This turned out to be very powerful for the students. They began literally to dream of the character in new situations, which drew them into new confrontations and adventures. Many dreamed of other characters as well, and large stretches of the story. This felt like confirmation of the universal nature of that material.

Small moments took on large significance when an actor fought the action, or was devastated by the action. We would stop and delve into it. I'd ask everyone in the class to do the scene that leads up to and ends in that moment. We'd all talk about what feelings erupted there, for everyone. To see the universality of the response, and the individual variations, was very important for everyone, especially for the actor carrying that role, and especially for me.

Sometimes the actors brought a wonderful, fresh interpretation that I kept. Sometimes I insisted on the original attitudes and subtle shadings. I never wrote down the exact lines of dialog. I felt it was important to have the scene unfold anew each time, no one knowing exactly what would come out next.

In the following semester the class continued as rehearsals for a scheduled opening of the play. The actors had evolved into their roles, and these stayed the same. We began working on the framework of the improvisation: how long the scene should take, where the dramatic peak was and how high, the tempo of the parts of the scene. A key scene, a cocktail party that goes surreal, had a lot of simultaneous action in it, so we spent time on the skills of directing the audience's focus. A three-piece band volunteered to play live accompaniment, and they began to work with us.

When it came to the actual performances, most of the audience was seated on pillows in the midst of the action. There were also a few rows of standard seats for those who preferred a more traditional experience. There were several stages scattered around, one five feet high with steps leading up to it, but the others were more subtle, ten-foot round stages, only nine inches off the floor. Actors often entered the action from a seat in the audience near their first stage. Audience members didn't know who was in the cast, and some even thought they were welcome to join in themselves. One lifted a glass from the cocktail table and enjoyed a drink (of colored water).

In the final scene the dreamer searches for the "miracle" everyone is talking about. She tries to follow others but finds they are all going in different directions. She steps into a shaft that propels her upwards through a primordial ooze where she's buffeted by evolutionary creatures. She emerges wounded and half blind. She gropes her way into a circle of people—everyone in the cast plus, to my surprise, at least half the audience. They stretched their faces up to be touched by the dreamer as she passed. She asked for a spot to sit in, but finally realizes she stands alone in the circle. She is the miracle.

The play often ended in silence rather than applause, more ritual than performance. It seemed to work its magic on the viewers. One philosophy professor commented afterwards that it was an interesting modern allegory, much like *Pilgrim's Progress*. Two days later he told me it had a delayed impact, that he'd dreamed vivid images not only from the play but from his life as well. He looked shaken.

A young student told me she saw the play three times. The first time she was filled up with the images of act one. The second evening she took in act two, and the third, act three. Each night she dreamed vividly. For many other young people the play became a participatory rite of passage; they had no problem following the story beneath the shifting imagery, at least intuitively if not intellectually.

This experiment convinced me that one person's archetypal imagery can touch others in a deep and meaningful way. But then isn't this the message of all art?

The Worm

After the play, it was a time of accolades. *The Dream* had touched many and left some looking—not within, but *at* me.

And then I dreamed that I was the puppet master sitting behind a giant face on a huge stage. The face sat atop a tower of a body. I had to work the controls to make it walk and gesture and open its mouth, while speaking its "wisdom." I was exhausted. I wanted to climb out. I wanted to be a normal size, a normal person. I slipped while trying to climb out and fell onto the stage, a naked little insignificant worm.

How many times in my life have I fallen to this naked worm stage? It is a regular part of my cycle. From where I sit now, again a naked worm, I can see that it is the very heart of my spiritual cycle. An evangelical conversion experience must be like this. I am a lowly sinner, now ready to live my life truthfully and right. It's the turning point in AA: I'm blowing it with my life and I need that Higher Power to help me through.

At the beginning of Quakerism George Fox encouraged people to "stand still in the Light," to let themselves be seen through and through, by themselves and by "God and everybody." This is the feeling of the worm.

We live such puffed-up lives; at least I find myself drifting into that place where I'm made up of my professional image, my competence, my ability to double-task my way through a complex life. All it takes is one of life's surprises to trip me up and expose my wormhood.

Germinating Seeds

I believe that when we actively participate in the interaction between mind and image we accelerate the process of becoming whole, we move toward our own wisdom. Jung identifies the inner dreamer as the only source of objective insight about ourselves. The dreamer knows us better than we do. The dreamer is not caught in subjective distortion. It sees us as someone else would, but far clearer because it can *really* see us. What an invaluable resource.

However, not everyone remembers their dreams. I wanted to design a workshop that evoked imagery. I wanted it to startle the unconscious into a response and ask the participant to express it so directly, so quickly that the mind had no chance to censor, alter, or add to the image itself. So I created the "Image Workshop," which ran for several years at the expressive arts cluster school with a changing repertoire of exercises.

Early in the class, exercises were designed to loosen people up. Risk and experiment, even goofiness, were fruitful qualities; there were no right or wrong responses. Instead there were rich and surprising responses, or else familiar material. I asked people to become animals or household appliances, and then people with those qualities. While they conversed with one other person, I'd have them age drastically, or change sex, or trade personalities with the other person. They'd get a last minute secret or objective to deal with. I wanted them to stretch their concept of "who I am," be willing to act out the other "me's" they carried within.

In another exercise people acted out their whole lives in 60 minutes. They'd be a group of friends, first on the playground at four years old, then 14. Then all would jump to 24, 55, and finally 70. No one knew what age they'd be next until I announced it. They didn't know what had happened to them until asked by a friend. One student told me many years later she still remembered stepping onto that four-year-old's playground with her feet apart and hands on hips, trying desperately to police the chaos around her. This image had a profound impression on her, and helped her ease her strict and judgmental side.

Many exercises were done in a circle. In one each person made a Tarot card of a painful or transforming event or truth. One picture and one title on a 3x5 card. These were then shuffled and passed out for someone else to relate to and express as if it were their own. This expression often involved the telling of a story. Others were encouraged to act or dance the story as it was being told. Sometimes there was musical accompaniment. The original author of the card saw the universality of his/her experience, how deeply and easily it fit someone else's experience. They were not alone. Several students commented on how terrifying it was to reveal that first truth to the circle, and what a revelation to have it understood and made into a universal human experience.

The "final exam" for the class was a party, held off campus in someone's home, where everyone was to choose the part of themselves they took too seriously, spoof it, costume it, and come to the party in that character, while I filmed it. We had among us an innocent angel, Joe Cool in blackface, a motley fool, a mountaintop guru, a nurse/caretaker, and more. These characters unfolded in their interactions. They discovered the restrictions, the ridiculousness of their dominant image in a way they themselves could laugh at. They discovered how that character limited them.

The woman who was the fool said it came from a fear of making a fool of herself. Afterwards she played the fool "for at least a year, maybe more (maybe the rest of my life) .... It was a huge opening in my life. I now say that if I have any wisdom at all, I learned it by being foolish."

This whole process was, among other things, quick and dirty therapy, being guided by a rank amateur in psychology. I did worry about unearthing something too big to deal with, but that never happened. Somehow our loving and playful circle handled everything with ease. We once stopped to hold a sobbing student, rocked and sang to her, allowed and accepted her reactions. Afterwards we picked up again with someone else's image and drew that woman back into community.

One student told me that other expressive arts faculty asked her to discover who she was and express it. She wanted to do that, but hadn't the foggiest idea how to go about it. The image workshop gave her tools and a flood of images to work with. This series of exercises gave people a visible cast of characters who were themselves—turned inside out, seen, understood, and loved for who they were. The rest of the group laughed and cried in recognition, grateful for one another's honesty.

But the workshop was not meant to be therapy. It was art training, learning to follow the lead of inner promptings. The images that flow from the inner voice can be wiser and truer than the tired old explanations of the mind. The inner voice is full of new material, things we don't know yet but are ready to know. What a difficult area to explore in a university setting.

We didn't talk about the exercises in class afterwards. I don't really know if that was because I didn't know how or because I wanted to fill the time with the exercise itself, and leave the talking for outside of class. I wanted people to carry the images they discovered the way we carry dreams around. They are complete in themselves, mysterious, germinating within like seeds with years worth of meaning growing gradually out of them. I was aiming us all, myself included, toward a mythical view of our lives.

At the time, though, I was struggling to understand and find my way.

A psych major, who seemed bound by his intellect, enrolled in the image workshop class. He asked me what was the point of all this stuff, why was I asking people to do it. I had none of the explanations and understandings that I have now. I couldn't answer, and I felt stupid. I was doing an intuitive dance, while he wanted analysis and lecture. He dropped the class, but by then the damage was done. I doubted myself and that whole track. I stopped offering the workshop, to many people's disappointment, I'm sure.

Other explorations of image continued, however. I found myself wondering if the images of my dreams could be valuable as isolated images out of any sequential order. I decided to create a Tarot deck where each dream was reduced to an image and a brief title. Once again I wondered how to determine the range. Where should I start and stop the cycle? And could I determine which images were archetypal? Would those images have significance for me at a different time in my life? have significance for someone else?

In the end, I gave up all the worry and followed an intuitive path. Any dream I liked got a card. I'd often get the title first and write it on the bottom. I'd gaze at the blank card until—sometimes—an image would appear. From there it was a simple step to draw and color it. Sometimes it was more of a thought process. I used the guideline of finding the heart of the dream by looking for the release of emotion. As the Jungians assert, the stirring of the emotions is a stirring of the archetype.

At one point I tested the effect of my own dream images as Tarot symbols for the purpose of drawing a picture of the whole of my life at that time. I laid out a formal Tarot reading and found it so powerful and emotional that I folded it up again immediately, without the usual milking of the images for meaning. This project remains incomplete to this day. There are now thirty more years of material I could include, but I doubt I'll return to that project. It did inspire a few individual Tarot decks by some students.

The Brain—A Dim Bulb

All my life I've worked to prompt the expression of truths that are still unknown. These truths don't come from the brain. The brain, after all, is not the brightest bulb in the box. Images come leaping out of us that enlighten us, that provide food for thought for years to come. The brain works well with the material, but the raw material is mined from the unconscious in the form of imagery. Scientists and inventors acknowledge that the image that formed the "Aha!" realization appeared to them in deep meditation or dreams. It came from elsewhere as an answer to their carefully researched question.

Revelatory images from the unconscious are not valued in our culture. We don't understand or acknowledge the importance of that special kind of mental activity that fosters the leap of imagery. Rational thinking marches forward in reliable ways, and is so important to many kinds of planning and activity. But lateral thinking, which slips easily sideways when straight ahead is not productive (or even exciting), is the key to all manner of problem solving. Lateral thinking notices things in the periphery, things that don't fit the pattern, things left by the wayside.

Taking a walk with my mother always took forever, because she noticed everything, and found beauty in it. "Oh, look!" she'd say and squat down to examine a mushroom. If you were anxious to reach your goal it could be very frustrating. She had that openness to the world of a two-year-old. Many of us learn to appreciate this quality from our little children. We stop and see again, as we haven't since we were two. The artist presents us with that mushroom in all its glory. When there's a frame around it and it's hung in a place of honor, or when it's painted in a way that transforms it into light or earthiness, we see and learn to love it, love the world again.

Even more valuable, the artist dares to express the inexplicable, the unacceptable truth as s/he experiences it. That first naming of a new thing opens up new territory for the rest of us to follow.

Called by Name

This morning I was called by name, in my dream. It was a whispered female voice that I thought was of a friend, though I couldn't see her. I was sledding down city streets on a little cardboard or plastic thing, propelled purely by my intention. I was racing against several others. We shot into the tunnel, me in the lead, the others close on my heels. I was rocketing along too close to the concrete pillars and had to swerve around them, much more complex driving than my earlier straight shots. Then I heard the voice, clear and soft in all that din. "Lynn. Lynn Waddington." I looked around the rafters for a friend watching the race. I said, "Hello friend. I hear you."

For some reason, I pushed myself along with my hands to gain more speed, even though I was still in the lead. It was a mistake. It slowed me down. The sled behind me caught up and clipped me on the way past. I spun sideways. The next sled clipped me worse and spun me farther. I wondered if this was the end, would I be mangled by one collision after another? I used my faltering intention to spin out of the way toward the side. The rest shot past me without collision. But my intention was spent, exhausted. I couldn't go anywhere. Was this the end? I wondered—a different kind of end?

When telling the dream to Margaret, mention of the whispered voice brought raw, vulnerable tears. And again when sidelined without the intention to move, I could barely speak it. Is this the end? But haven't I been sidelined for a year now? My rocketing days seem long gone. If not, in what ways am I still rocketing? If this is a Divine call, what is God calling me to? I have to admit, it was a little hard to recognize as God because it was a female voice. It certainly was a still, small voice amidst the storm. It was as personally directed as my experience on the lawn as a child. It carried an immense amount of emotion that I was utterly vulnerable to.

Many years ago I dreamed that I was walking along a hospital corridor with a tall, elegant woman. She was remarkable for her poise and intelligence and compassion. Every now and then she would pause our conversation to enter a room and see a patient for a few moments. One of these patients was on monitors, I could tell from the hall, because the alarms went off while she was there. She calmly left the room to resume our journey. I realized she was Death, visiting these patients to ease them through the transition.

So it is not the Grim Reaper in a black hood who is my companion, but this woman walking beside me on my journey. The compassionate reaper. I would trust her and go with her.

Is the whispered voice the death figure I met in the hospital dream, telling me my time is near or here? Is she God calling me to be about my true business, Her business? I thought I was already doing just that, or at least as close as I can discern. At the very least this dream calls me to listen, think, and write with greater integrity.

It's pretty presumptuous to think these writings are a divine calling. That makes the work so precious I can hardly proceed. Rather, I want to simply write what's important to me, and not write anything unimportant. That's something I think I can do, though even that is not as easy as it sounds. At this point I have no idea how things might come together into a coherent whole.

I keep chiding myself for not doing the things that are important to others. I almost never take time aside to meditate or pray, except through this writing or the sculpting of the Stone Age females. These activities bring my heart and mind and hands together in a blessed harmony. I carry loved ones around in my heart, trying to keep the loving stronger than the fretting. It seems to open the channel for God's love to flow along with mine. It's probably all the same love anyway.

I don't read inspirational literature or scripture, or rather my inspiration comes from unusual places: a good novel, a stunning photograph, a friend's offhand comment. And of course from these remarkable images from within, from the Other within, which haunt me, if I let them. This morning's whispered call is certainly one such.

As so often happens, this brush with the Powerful comes without answers. It offers something else. Is it a question? A hint? Somehow it is careful to not let me dismiss it by figuring out what the answer would be, and then stashing it away in the mind's files. It's meant to follow me as I walk through my days. That spin onto the sidelines in the dream is meant to stop me so I can be haunted by that whispered voice. Today I will cancel plans, stay close, and listen.

What am I called to do? If God's business, what in the world might that be? And talk about presumption! "Doing God's business" has led many before me astray. It seems to lead straight to hubris and meddling in other people's lives. And watching these vaunted televangelists come crashing down to flawed personhood has led many of us to steer clear of the very notion of divine calling. Yet, central to Quakerism is being open to discerning God's leading—truly listening.

And yet all of life seems to be woven into a single fabric. What any of us does is not arbitrary, it's a part of that whole. If we can't see the whole, we also can't see our little part. I can't run around joining every worthy cause I believe in without exhausting myself. And don't I stay a follower while doing that? What is my unique contribution? I hope to heaven I was made this odd-duck way for *some* good reason.

I'm reminded of my stepson's early soccer games. Both teams of little boys would swarm to wherever the ball was, leaving the rest of the field deserted. No matter how hard the coach tried to get them to play their positions, the excitement was at the ball, and their eagerness sucked them there. My position seems to be way over here in a deserted area of the field right now, even though I too feel the tug toward the ball.

Like most everyone I know, I want to make the world a better place while I'm here. Surely my time would be better spent up at the hospital talking with other people who are also nearing death. And how can I hear if that's the thing to do? If I follow my impulse moment by moment, I stay here and write, and let myself get drawn back into sculpting more ancient figures. There is one that is calling me by name. She floats in my head, she delights me, intrigues me. What does she have to tell me? Her message is more question than answer, like the message of the whispered voice in the tunnel.

It's the lack of answers that makes me wonder if I'm on any useful path. Don't we just worship answers, though? Answers let us relax and feel good about ourselves, perhaps too readily at times. I'm from the branch of Quakers that has no creed. Perhaps the closest we come is an evolving set of queries that we use to measure how well we walk our talk. It's not what we say, what we believe, that is important. It's how we live our lives, let our lives speak for us.

This tends to encourage a life based on questions rather than answers. We are seekers, not finders. For every profound experience I've had, I've been left with deep questions. One of my earlier dreams was an encounter with the wise woman, a kind of guru on the mountaintop, but with flowing robes, lush nature, and vibrant energy. She had a handful of pearls to give me. I was deeply honored. She then grinned and flung them out and down the mountain.

So how do I find them, collect them in the shrubbery, if that's what I'm to do? Or am I simply to seek them? Or simpler still, to glimpse them, and let them belong to the natural world? The pearls may be the answer, but the gift is in the process, the journey. I clearly don't get to carry them around in my pocket. I'm the seeker, not the holder.

So I stay here at the keyboard, seeking patterns, meanings and directions. I stay here this morning because I'm drawn here. Can I really stay true enough to follow the lead moment to moment? Perhaps I can because of this time in my life, close to my death. It's an experiment. I've wanted to live my whole life this way, so close to the Guide. Let's see what comes of it.

CHAPTER SIX

Step Into the Light: It Will Feel Like Love

Step Into the Light:
It Will Feel Like Love

Hey, Wait a Minute!

I can't write the queer coming out story for a gay audience and the epiphany for a religious audience. I've tried, and it's ruined both halves to be passed off as complete without the other half. The truth is, if we want a relationship with God, we need absolute personal integrity. That relationship begins with our relationship with our own truth. George Fox tells us to "stand still in the Light" and let it reveal everything, to us as well as to God. I was very fortunate to have this happen at a tender age, and to have the support of my mother. If I'd chosen the path of dishonesty and repression, I might have felt bigoted outrage at others having fun where I'd paid such a high price of discipline and sacrifice.

Talking about my androgyny with straight folks is usually a trial. One enlightened man with whom I share my inner journey translated my words into "the inner feminine." One of the words he used for feminine was "yielding." I suppose that's true, especially considering women's talent for creating community, where our rugged individualism must yield a bit in the face of the wisdom of the group.

But his words triggered a response from long ago as well, when women were defined by men, and so looked like all the repressed sides of the male persona. The old Jungian constructs ended up in ridiculous dichotomies: male/active, female/passive; male/conscious, female/unconscious! I used to think, listening to my Jungian shrink back in the '60s, "Hey, wait a minute! I'm active. I'm conscious!"

I look at my exhibit of Paleolithic and Neolithic reproductions, where virtually all of the human depictions are female, and wonder what the psyche looked like for them. The feminine principle was certainly not a shadow of the male. Most likely, women determined kinship, expanded the diet through their inventions of pots and grinding stones and cooking. They likely initiated sex and chose their partner or partners. They embodied the attributes of God: Creator and Source, the key to future generations and survival of the clan. In this, they were awesome and mysterious.

What quiet self-assurance we could carry within us if the feminine were honored. Perhaps I wouldn't have had to pretend I was a boy in order to express my courage and adventure and intellect.

Or perhaps we're all both halves. Look how hard our culture works to cram us into one half and erase all traces of the other half. Pink and blue from the cradle, school dress codes that insisted on skirts, even in freezing temperatures, long hair/short hair. I know I was on the more extreme end of the spectrum, visible because my mother allowed it. After all, we lived without neighbors and their reactions for many years. We also lived for many years without the bombardment of images from television. We were who we were in all our oddity.

Sex

I don't believe we can talk about the Spirit without also talking about sex. In spite of the severe damage we've inflicted on our sexual expression as a society, orgasm is still the commonest form of transcendence we know.

I believe sex was a part of Spiritual expression up until Old Testament times. It was certainly difficult to eradicate then. Now, the long-term suppression of sexual expression emerges in atrocities such as the Catholic priests' scandals.

Sex has been relegated to the gutter, as in the old admonition, "Get your mind out of the gutter!" "Fuck you" is the worst thing we can think to say to someone. How then can we possibly see God in this activity?

And then there's my childhood neighbor Charlie. Charlie suffered from cerebral palsy, to the degree that it was possible, but difficult, to understand his speech. Though he was a young adult he played with us, and enabled many projects to be built that we could never have accomplished by ourselves. Together we made an elaborate miniature golf course one summer, and a lawn-sized village with lights another year.

But one summer in my puberty Charlie called me into his house to help him with something when his elderly parents weren't there. He was our special friend. So when he beckoned me over I trusted him. What he showed me though was his bulging penis. He wrapped my hand around it and showed me what to do. I was afraid and fascinated. I also empathized with his dilemma of being too uncoordinated to do this for himself. But then he led me to his bed, pushed me backwards onto it and tugged my pants down enough to push himself into my crotch.

I adamantly didn't want this, but how to be rude to Charlie at this point after agreeing to everything so far? After treating him with special patience and respect for years. I squeezed my vagina shut so tight there was no way he could get in, at least at the pressure he was applying then. When he came I worried that some would get in and impregnate me. I still hadn't gotten angry at him. Now I felt weepy. He had ruined the friendship forever. Before he let me go he gave me a tube of his mother's lipstick and told me to let him know when it would fit inside me. Then he pulled all the change from his pocket and gave it to me.

I wanted to throw it at him along with the lipstick. I felt like a whore. How did that happen? I ran home and washed thoroughly. I avoided him, pretended to not hear him when he called to me. And who could I tell? We were all Charlie's champions. I found my own path of resistance and self-protection.

I tell this story because it is so common in the sexual experience of women. My sexual awakening was rude and traumatic. It had nothing to do with my pleasure, or even my permission. I was merely the agent of his release. Some men have wondered what the harm was—I wasn't wounded, I didn't become pregnant. It is so lonely and frightening to defend our fragile bodies from attack, to be alone in worrying about the life-altering consequences of pregnancy, to be denied the pleasure of mutual exploration. What I didn't know then was how large an impact that brief moment was to have on my life. When I married later, my husband's every sexual entry meant panic and pain for me. It took decades to unclench my vagina and even longer to achieve a vaginal orgasm. When I did it was accompanied by sobbing. Do men have any idea?

The legacy I carried with me far into adulthood was a terror of penetration, an instinctive clenching down in self protection, an inability to feel pleasure from intercourse. If one in four women has such a history, or a far worse one, what a huge loss of our birthright. And what a huge and baffling loss to the men who want to bring us to ecstatic pleasure and deep trust and communion with them.

In spite of my lesbian nature, which directed all my deepest longings toward select women friends, I accepted Jim's proposal of marriage. He was a nice guy, kind, playful, full of integrity, not really sexy, but able to get me hot and bothered. That was enough. Maybe marriage would fix me. In any case, spinsterhood was the only option I could see, and that seemed lonely and difficult.

Building a sexual relationship wasn't easy. Any suggestions I made so he could better please me were taken as criticism. He told me that it was my problem, I was frigid. Other women didn't complain that he was too rough with their breasts or too fast to orgasm. I knew he was right. I shouldn't have been trying to be a heterosexual. I carried a lot of inhibitions in my poor body. He and I both deserved a better fit.

I began graduate work in theater arts and came alive in that community. Once he and I arrived at a restaurant to find my theater friends at a huge table, including a woman playwright I was drawn to. I led us to the adjoining empty table, where he, poor guy, played second fiddle to these effervescent actors.

When we left I went on outside while he paid the bill. I wanted to stay with my friends. I dreaded the morose confrontation that was surely coming. I was striding up the block when he emerged. I heard him call after me, "Where do you think you're going?" Though I didn't know where yet, I realized I was going. We agreed to separate. I moved into an apartment with two other theater women, one the fascinating playwright. We became involved, though neither of us knew what we were doing. Her sister was an out lesbian who was delighted to introduce us to the hidden underground world she was part of.

Sexually we fumbled around eagerly but rather blindly, and in spite of greater familiarity and deeper trust, I remained "frigid." Her sister took us to a dyke weekend on the Russian River which set off such a longing and lust in me I was terrified. The dance music lodged permanently in my head. We both retreated from our scary venture, she into a straight marriage and I into a period of dating men. Ah, what a chicken I was.

I got a teaching job north of San Francisco. In the very first semester I fell for a tall, stunning student who was a lesbian. She returned my interest. We became involved, and when she heard of my sexual dysfunction she was determined to awaken me. She wouldn't accept my assurances that I was really OK with how I was, and of course, I wasn't OK, I was just afraid of trying and failing.

She listened closely enough to learn what turned me on and what shut me down. She never lost heart. She brought me to orgasm reliably enough to give me hope, to give me a new self-image. I learned to trust her, to throw caution to the winds, to experience wild abandon.

Until this time, my experience, and therefore the Human Experience was solitary. The barrier of our skin was absolute, impenetrable. I could bring others to fulfillment, and I could respond with warmth and gratitude, but my emotions were muted. Though she was hugely significant, she was not my soul mate. With subsequent partners I have journeyed deeper and deeper into the mysteries of communion, and especially with my current partner and true soul mate, Margaret.

One thing Margaret and I had in common was a history of sexual damage, and together we healed each other of the residue from that. For years my deep orgasm was followed by wrenching sobs. At first I wondered why I was sad. Then I saw it as cleansing, letting go. It has stopped now. Perhaps my body is finally at peace, whole.

In orgasm I can leave my solitary shell of a body and merge with my partner. I see her as so beautiful, feel her as the answer to my longing. I flow into her, and occasionally through her into the great void beyond. We speak so seldom about such things, and they are so hard to express that I don't know if I'm merely stating the obvious.

The Sixties Fulcrum

Just as my father's generation was deeply imprinted by the Depression, which happened in their young adulthood, my generation was deeply imprinted by the '60s. I don't hear people talking about it, nor do I talk about it. We're intimidated by the conservative backlash that is still with us. Those in public office or positions of responsibility are especially eager to deny its influence. We've heard "but I didn't inhale!" and "that was before I found Christ, or Ramakrishna." Where is the appreciation for the beautiful changes wrought by those drug years, that experiment in peace and joy, free love and creativity?

I walked a middle ground between the extremes, clearly on the side of the new and experimenting along with my students, but older, on the faculty, staying responsible, helping younger ones keep their feet on the ground. I was introduced to marijuana as a graduate student in San Francisco. An actor friend brought a joint over to my house. We sat facing each other on my couch. When I reported that nothing was happening, she asked what I was noticing and what I was thinking about. To my surprise both of these functions were heightened beyond my everyday norm, without my recognizing it.

I found I had an artist's vision of even the most mundane of things, the smoke rising from my cigarette, the plush of the lap robe. As we talked, there was the same acceptance and appreciation for the truth of our feelings and thoughts. I relaxed into a courage to speak my truth, and heard hers with empathy and recognition. Why shield myself from attack? What a silly waste of energy. My newly recognized truths were coming from a place deeper and farther from my protective wall than I'd dared to venture before, and so they came with the shock of humor. We laughed until the tears rolled down, until our cheeks hurt. Each shared revelation back and forth triggered a new round of laughter. That evening did not dissolve the next morning, as happens with a night at the bar. It changed my life.

I was married at the time, and my husband adamantly chose the straight path. He was not in this with me. Much as he loved Fats Waller, John Coltrane, and Lawrence Ferlinghetti, all of whose brilliance was released with chemical assistance, he believed we shouldn't need that crutch. Perhaps we shouldn't, but I found I needed some kind of help to pry myself out of the rigid '50s. The '60s looked to me like the whole forest had suddenly burst into bloom. I couldn't imagine looking at it through the '50s window; I had to run through it and roll around in the fallen blossoms. It was a sensory feast.

It was also a creative artist's dream. An overheard conversation in a restaurant, a rocking chair in the sun became the raw material for plays and paintings. Inner images rolled out effortlessly to meet the offered gems of the world, and both hit home in the heart.

Gateway into This World

Preparing for my daughter's home birth, I knew without consciously knowing that I would create a Gateway between the worlds in that little bedroom. I wanted to feel safe. In addition to the baby's father, Ray, I invited five people to sit vigil. Perhaps more accurately, to stand sentinel. I didn't know what I would encounter, but it felt as though I was about to round the horn in a clipper ship and might have to brave the fiercest winds on Earth.

My dear friend Barbara was easy. She was my primary helper throughout my life. Her calm eye would assess the situation and supply what was called for throughout. My sister-in-law Jane was there willy-nilly, because she was my guest, traveling through from the Philipines, where she'd assisted and apprenticed to a famous psychic healer. My colleague Elizabeth had just played me in a version of *The Dream*. She was somehow me in a much more vulnerable state, buffeted but seeing clear, a gifted poet reporting from the storm.

Lawrence, a student not much younger than I was, had the air of a dignified gentleman with a devilish glint. I'd be a lot like him if I'd been born male. Did he bring a camera or pick up Ray's? Whichever, he gave up the pure witness of the Gateway for the service of documenting it.

And Mac, the most mysterious invitation of all, why did I want him there? I hadn't bared much of my soul to him ever. He'd been one of the initiators of the expressive arts cluster school. He played the clown, the fool, dancing elusively through our negotiations with the administration. He held true to only that tiny patch of here and now that he knew to be true. He surfed that unknown venture with a focus that pinned us to a safe center and jettisoned everything unnecessary. I wanted that.

I can see now from the pictures the awesomeness of that event. My circle of sentinels held this side of the Gateway open. I could hear them gathering receiving blankets and boiling scissors. They allowed me to slide farther down the opening toward that other world, to go to meet this child closer to the Gateway. I now understood the indifference that cats and dogs showed to my presence at their birthings.

As a little child I'd witnessed several birthings. Our cat was rather prolific, giving us a new litter every year. Her preferred spot was under the corner cupboard, a deep cave with a low roof. We supplied her with soft bedding which she rucked up into a nest. The four of us kids would spread out on our stomachs with our faces to the front edge of her cave to watch. She ignored us. Perhaps we felt like her sentinels. I watched puppies and a calf emerge, saw death and deformity—these things are part of country life, part of what Mother thought important to our education.

Some weeks or months before I was due, Barbara's shepherd-wolf mix decided to deliver her pups on my back porch. I sat vigil again and studied her process very carefully. The Lamaze classes had us pant. Her panting was so matter-of-fact and cheerful. Her contractions made her very uncomfortable; she couldn't figure out whether to lie, sit or stand. Eventually, it was the movement from one to the other that was crucial. She would struggle to rise and drop a pup, almost leave it behind.

I knew I wanted to squat rather than lie on my back, and on the baby's head. Now I saw that the squat blended into the rising to all fours, like the wolf. The wolf moved into my body and stretched the mammalian birth roots of this experience way back.

Heart Chakra

It is a powerful, archetypal force that draws us together in love. This happens with our children and with our deepest friendships as well as with our mates. There is a deep recognition of the value of this connection, long before our conscious minds can explain what's going on. We are drawn into deep soul work. This person can teach us what we need to learn. This person will melt our crusty boundaries. This person can see and love the potential "me" within, thereby helping me fulfill that promise. This person glows with such inner beauty that I can't help but give my heart in love. Love leads us, and we follow.

I'm back from a week of basking in my granddaughter's presence, hours spent holding her tiny form against my chest. Her slightest fussiness calms right down when we go chest to chest, heart to heart. My own fussiness calms down too. I don't really have anything more important to do than this. My heart melts. She lays her tiny hands on me, on either side of her head, and I am content.

When you fall in love with someone, you want to press your chest against theirs. It feeds the heart like nothing else. Both hearts. I remember seeing the sun blazing out of my chest one day long ago in a mystical experience while walking the concourse at an airport. Thomas Merton saw this too. He said, "There is no way of telling people that they are walking around shining like the sun..." Little Genevieve is shining already; she was from the moment she was born, I'm sure. How powerful a force field that must be when two chests beam into each other. No wonder we love to hug each other so much.

We like to think of light as an image for clarity, intelligence. We forget sometimes the other side of fire—heat, warmth—images of passion, of love.

Way Opens, Way Closes

Love, like work, is one of God's callings into Her/His deep journey. Love can transform us and a bit of the world as well.

I'd fallen in love several times, thinking each time that this one could last. It seemed to me that serial monogamy was the true nature of human relations. That a person could "speak to my condition" for a specific period of my life, and then we'd grow apart. Literally, grow in different directions, directions I couldn't follow, but which were clearly right for the other.

I was willing to throw my heart into a relationship, plumb the depths of our truths, take risks, help each other out, travel a more or less joint path for as long as it was fruitful for both of us. We did not break up to avoid difficulties, as the magazines suggest. It was more like we'd finished our graduate studies, and were now drawn to careers as diverse as Wiccan ritual and international trade.

The dissolutions were for the most part amicable. The primary difficulties came from cultural expectations. We now had what the magazines call a "failed marriage" or "broken home." Clearly, someone must be at fault. We must have done something wrong. To muddy the picture, there were often mistakes and hurtful moments, but I'm not convinced, looking back at those liaisons, that doing it better would have resulted in our still thriving together now, twenty or thirty years later.

And much as we hate to admit it, we're sometimes called out of relationship as well as to it. Way not only opens, way also closes at times. I see divorce not as a modern tragedy but as a major step forward. The tragedies happen around the edges with finances, custody, and visitation.

Other cultures, now and in the past, have created viable alternative solutions to all these needs. And I seem to have a lot of friends who've had a monogamous first part of life until the children were older or emancipated. At that point both partners seem happy to move on to a relationship that better stirs the soul.

How much of the intensity around this discussion comes from our clinging to monogamy as the natural human pattern? Monogamy is designed to assure the paternity of the children and provide wifely services for the husband on the one hand, and on the other to assure financial security and a dad-figure for the children. It seems to me that serial monogamy is the true nature of human relations.

To say that the love has simply shifted toward friendship or a working partnership or even silent and non-abusive cohabitation, but is still love, is to ignore the reasons for loving someone. Without the mutual baring of souls, sharing of struggles and joys, and support for each other it is a sorry kind of love indeed. Why is the continuation of an empty partnership preferable to a vibrant exchange?

A Wedding?

When I fell in love with Margaret, who is also a Quaker, it was like coming home. I finally understood why early Quakers were so adamant about marrying another Quaker. Subtle values and ethics were shared at last, with no real temptation toward little lapses and white lies.

Her teen and almost-teen sons suggested we get married. We were far from sure that we wanted a ceremony at all. Why not take the greatest adventure of all and live life day to day, true to the Inner Guide? Of course we wanted what I suppose everyone wants—a mutually nurturing relationship we both thrive and grow in, that lasts forever. We just weren't sure that marriage had much to do with it. Did those vows really make any difference? But their point was compelling. Weren't we married in essence? Wouldn't it be the greater integrity to bring it to Quaker Meeting, make it public?

Margaret was once again braver than I about going public. Her sense of personal integrity has always pushed her to accept the challenge of walking her talk. Her ties to community were very strong. I admired that in her and wanted to trust her lead.

Public has been difficult for me. Loving a woman across these decades of homophobia, growing acceptance, and backlash is something best kept quiet. My times of loving a man in those decades brought lots of praise and encouragement, while loving a woman brought silence.

Coming out has happened in stages, at least for me. The creeping awareness within myself took many years. After all, that was the fifties, and there was no one out there like me then, as far as I knew. Then in the '60s admitting my attraction to an individual woman was a huge and frightening step. Calling myself one of those despised names was very difficult.

I came out to my mother, expecting to then tell the whole family, but she said, "don't tell Dad, he couldn't handle it," which raised the whole question of which family members *do* I tell. Someone in my California Quaker Meeting tried to convince me it was safe among them, but I didn't quite trust that. I was carefully closeted at work, so as not to impact my finances. Can you see what a checkerboard of lies and truth this creates?

How could I live a life of integrity with this huge area an exception to the rest? Because it was about my intimate sex life it was supposedly nobody else's business. But it was also about my entire home life, far too much to leave out.

A big public wedding would be the ultimate coming out. Could I stand it? I'd been screamed at in the street by a neighbor for being a "lesbian whore." Perhaps this public declaration could erase that wound. We could at least invite beloved friends and family from long ago and far away to join with our current community. How that would heal my fractured life! In the end we were overwhelmed by how many came, flying in from across the country. Not only siblings but aunts and cousins, not only my daughter's longtime boyfriend but also his family.

After a lifetime of hiding my loves to some degree, my open and public declaration of love for Margaret left me feeling completely vulnerable. We stood together to say our vows, intimate in this very public setting, all my protection stripped away.

There were people there who knew me through some of my most difficult times, my gangly teens and bumbling twenties, my bad relationships and bad habits. They'd seen me, and here they were supporting me with their love. I watched these people from the fragmented eras of my life, laughing and talking with each other, knitting together my fractured soul.

All those years of wishing for another grand mystical experience like the one in my adolescence—and here it was, brought to me by these people who were my beloved family. They saw me and loved me, as God had done. I was defenseless and profoundly touched.

Till Death Do Us Part—Not

Our first challenge in preparing for the wedding was with the traditional Quaker vows, in essence: ". . . I take thee . . . to be my [spouse] promising, with Divine Assistance, to be unto thee a loving and faithful [spouse] so long as we both shall live." The especially troubling part was "so long as we both shall live." We appreciated the intention, but a vow is not a statement of intention, it's a promise to carry out, no matter what. With our history of broken relationships this vow looked like an invitation to break another promise, or else to stay in a bad situation we hadn't anticipated and couldn't turn to good use. Is it *always* best to stay together? It hadn't been before. Margaret especially was determined to not have to break her word again. She has lived with more integrity than anyone else I've ever known. I'm still learning from her every day as she thinks through and chooses the path of integrity where others, like me, can't even see where custom is asking us to be less than true. If one lives with integrity, then the promise of forever would have to take precedence over any other Divine call. For me, the call comes first.

We became very aware that there are things one can promise and things one can't. We couldn't promise to love forever, either. Love is a gift, a blessing visited upon us. It comes out of nowhere and takes us over. It leads us into our deepest and most valuable adventures. It is the stuff of God, and therefore not under our control. Sometimes love goes, as mysteriously as it comes. It is a gift from God, after all.

The real question for our marriage was what *can* we promise and carry out that will foster and shelter love, cause it to grow and engage us in its challenges? These were the things we wanted to promise each other. We brainstormed a very long list, trying to name the trouble spots where special focus was needed.

That night I couldn't sleep. I sat up playing with the list to find its core. It worked on me as hard as I was working on it. The list fell into groupings and got more clear and simple until four promises emerged: to be honest and faithful, to care for her well-being, to take her family as my own, and to help her answer God's call in her life. We lived with these for a while and found them to be central. Everything else was included in these.

The first, and most fundamental of the promises, was to be honest and faithful. Whatever happened, we'd want to be on the same side of the fence, working on it together. It would be to each other that we risked baring our soul. We'd have to trust that we were loved for who we are. We didn't want to gripe to outsiders, or follow an allure to an easier love on the side. On this promise we could build trust.

Second was to care for each other's well-being, staying aware of each other's difficulties and helping. To do our share of the scut work. To translate high-fallutin' ideals into practical action. To see what the other needs that she isn't quite aware of yet, and offer to help. To nurse each other through illness and trauma.

Third was to take each other's family as our own. That meant a huge challenge for me in helping to raise her two sons. I had a daughter, but sons were new, siblings were new, and resentment toward a stepmother was new. Our learning to live with one another happened through their adolescence, not an easy time. The rest of the merging of families went well and in some cases delightfully.

The fourth and final vow was to help each other answer God's call in her life. How many times had I felt that my spiritual call was at odds with my partner and his or her wishes? This conflict does not bode well for the partner, because, in my case, the call always wins out. As I still feel it should. So we were determined to place it at the center of our relationship; wherever each might be called, and even if it seemed not to include the other, we would help each other rather than resist.

What in my life experience brought me to the importance of these particular promises?

TO BE MY PARTNER

Partner is a reminder of our equality. We're yoked as oxen in this endeavor, free to speak up about our limitations and our wishes, working together on a joint quest that has the potential to transform each of us through our interaction with the other.

WITH DIVINE ASSISTANCE

Marriage feels like a divine assignment. Love clobbers us and draws us into this adventure. I realize I've grown as much as I can as a solitary individual. I have to open my heart, see myself as I am seen. We have to learn to love each other for who we truly are, as God loves us. When the courageous path seems daunting, I remember God seemed to call me to it. I can ask for clarity and help.

HONESTY

Being honest is the only way we know we are loved. If it's not me, but some idealized version of me, that you love, it's not going to touch my soul. I can still believe myself unlovable. I have to show you the secrets of my heart—my own secrets—and then see myself as you see me. I have to hear from the depths of your heart and learn how that opens me.

Once, being told off became a major mystical experience for me. One evening my lover came home and said, "We have to have a talk," which, between lovers, really hits the dread button. My muscles tightened, my stomach gripped; I armed myself with all my good intentions, extra efforts, the wrongs I'd suffered. I launched off strenuously with "I never intended…" which she answered with "intentions aside, this is how you behaved."

I saw her soul.

My defenses crumbled. I actually let myself take in what she said. The pain of embarrassment became irrelevant. Her words became like Light, shining into me. I saw the source of Light in her—no, through her; no, maybe behind or beyond her—yet beaming into me. Cleansing me like the Refiner's Fire. I had no more need to do those thoughtless things. I wanted to be the caring person I assumed I was.

It takes such courage to say what I need, what I'm afraid of. It feels as though I'm risking the whole relationship. There's such overwhelming relief when she hears and takes it on as something we can both work on.

If you would find a spark of love anew, drop into greater honesty.

FAITHFULNESS

To be faithful is the basis of trust, and the promise to go on the journey together with your partner. There are more ways to betray trust than having an affair, though this is the cruelest, perhaps because it's the most intimate and intense. To keep intimacy alive we need to listen to each other deeply enough to see that each is struggling along the road to the same fulfillment or enlightenment.

We need to hold very tenderly the damage most of us carry into adulthood. My sexual abuse left me well defended and therefore very far from the sweet abandon that is the goal of intimacy. This journey called for deep trust. A little lightweight, uncomplicated sex on the side can be very appealing.

And indeed, both partners have to be willing to undertake a journey that involves them both, with all their uniqueness and damage. Those who are discovering a truer sexual identity than what was once foisted on everyone may need to undertake the journey with someone more appropriate. Many, though, are in fertile ground where they are; they haven't ever opened those deeper doors. While counseling can be a huge help, there are parts of the journey together that only tender acceptance can heal.

There is also a conversational unfaithfulness. Those things that are the hardest to say, that can drop a marriage to new depths, are easy to say to an outsider. They come out as complaints and jokes even. And the marriage suffers another setback. Often talking to a trusted friend is a good way to get clear about what your truth is, but this needs to be taken back to the marriage.

Build trust by being faithful. Do what you say and say what you've done.

CARE

In the giving and receiving of tender care comes love. Whichever you do less of, if you would foster love, do more.

Caring for each other's well-being is all about the daily nitty-gritty of life. The most important part of this one was its mutuality. I wanted to do for Margaret the things I did best and the things that needed doing.

I wanted the confidence that she'd do that for me. This was the one that traditional marriage vows called "in sickness and in health." We had many imbalances, but they went both ways, and the upshot was that it felt perfectly balanced.

That is, until I got sick. For a year now I've been struggling with terminal pulmonary fibrosis and a disabling muscle wasting as well. Most of the time I can't cook meals, drive to the grocery store, make the bed, go to work, wash the car, water the garden. Instead, I'm an additional burden. I need a wheelchair hauled out of the trunk, assembled and pushed. I need the water bottle on my oxygen concentrator refilled. Margaret is now working full time, coming home to her chores, my chores and my maintenance, and around the edges doing her correspondence and soul work.

It's a different kind of difficult for me. It's very hard for me to be so helpless, to have to ask for help. I'd rather refill my water glass any day than ask someone to do it for me, especially Margaret, who's doing so much already. We try to spread the care around to a care committee of ten and circle of friends beyond that. Being on the receiving end of meals and flowers and prayers is very wonderful! But to continue receiving and give so little back is not easy. I've had to find a different way to express my care. I reach out by words now a lot, both spoken and written.

FAMILY

I take thy family as my own. Margaret's parents were easy; I already loved them. We'd bonded in a special way years before while we were in the same Quaker Meeting. Her sons were another matter. When we met they were seven and eleven years old and that was totally new territory for me. Unfortunately, enough of what was going on was kept from them that they saw me as the villain who broke up their happy home.

We'd ended the other relationships as cleanly and harmoniously as we could. This was possible primarily because it was our partners, and not us, who'd moved on to a new passion. If anyone were to feel wronged it would be us. But for both of us—all four of us—it seemed clear that the spark of joint adventure and mutual growth had been gone for quite a while. I can't say that there was no pain from the broken trust. But then each of us, in a rebound position, was captivated by the other, and pain was pretty much forgotten.

But I had no skills in the parenting techniques these boys were used to. It was a difficult time, with some wonderful moments, running through their adolescence. But this was clearly the challenge for me, and clearly necessary for us to engage in. Time and maturation thankfully have healed the hurts.

My daughter was already emancipated. And over the years we've helped her wrestle with the difficulties of young adulthood.

THE CALL

In my earlier years I tried several relationships that all seemed to end in the same dilemma. This person had little understanding of my inner drive to follow the Guide. I was unable to stay true to each because they seemed on divergent paths. I felt that I had to choose over and over again between answering my call and carrying on in that relationship. The call always won. In a showdown between a lover and a Spiritual leading, the lover usually does not fare very well.

What I wanted was someone who wouldn't see my call as a threat, someone who'd actually encourage, help.

On April 13, 1996, we spoke these vows to each other in a Meeting for Worship with 200 dear friends and family present.

I take thee to be my beloved partner, promising with Divine assistance to remain honest and faithful, to care for thy well-being, to take thy family as my own, and to help thee answer God's call in thy life.

These vows have stood us in such good stead. We have a morning ritual of sitting up in bed with our tea and sharing our dreams, our thoughts, the new insights that have come overnight, our plans, and easy comments on the dahlias and rabbits and deer and fog outside our window. Into this open space can come the things that are hard to say, hard to become aware of even. We stay clean and up to date with each other in this daily ritual.

I was especially focused on keeping equality in our caring for each other's well-being. But when I buckled under the multiple illnesses and the burden of care became so much more Margaret's than mine, it pleased me no end to take over replacing her antiquated computer and moving her valuable work from one to the other. This I can do, at least with a little phone help, and it was a task that seemed beyond reach to her.

Once we were sitting across from each other in a large circle. I saw her sit up in alarm, like a dog that's heard something beyond our hearing range. She slipped around the outside of the circle and checked my oxygen tank. Sure enough, it was empty. She moved the regulator over to the spare tank. I hadn't begun to feel the effects of no oxygen yet, but she knew. She is, of course, kind and considerate even without those vows, but the vows have served to make us conscious of the value of these little daily acts of caring.

At this very moment, the older of our two sons is getting married. I will stop writing and focus my blessings on him and his beloved. I hope they can find the divine mystery that enters the heart when one commits to protecting that precious gift that is love.

A Marriage of Solitudes

All my life I've been a solitary and "independent" person. A perceptive teacher wrote in my high school evaluation that I was "*too independent*"—I was outraged. That was like saying I was too creative. Alas, it's been a long road toward trusting *inter*dependence.

The thing about being a little odd, like queer and a visionary, is that all my life lessons seemed to be encouraging me to be a loner. It fit the rugged individualism that is our national ideal anyway.

Someone once asked me what was the difference between spirit and soul. It was clear to me then that spirit was one's relationship with God and soul was one's relationship with other people. I'd say now that my life had lots of spirit and almost no soul in it.

I was so busy protecting myself that my human relationships suffered. They always took a back seat to my spiritual path. They rarely lasted more than a couple of years.

With Margaret I felt a deeper resonance. Perhaps it is our shared religious background, both of us raised in Quaker families. Perhaps it was significant that I was 50 and wiser. Perhaps it just took me until then to find a suitable lesbian Quaker partner. It is a very limited pool, somewhat reminiscent of a tiny, isolated Siberian village for a straight teenager.

Whatever it was, we felt like an old married couple from the beginning. We cooked for each other and sat by the fire with our books and spoke of our spiritual journeys. We listened deep truths out of each other. I felt this one might really be different.

I longed for, and found in Margaret, a partner who recognized the spiritual call as one's highest obligation. If she were called to China to found a clinic, I would help her go, not try to hold her back. We both knew a commitment to supporting each other in this way would be a real challenge, and hoped that by recognizing and naming it, by promising it, we'd be able to carry it out. We were determined.

What has taken me years to recognize is the importance of making this spiritual journey a shared endeavor. God's work for me is part of a larger plan that includes family and friends working on closely related callings, kindred spirits I've never met but connect with through the Internet and large organizations, even those of my generation who've lived through the same national and global turning points. We are all emerging into the new world together, each with our own unique little contributions.

My old image of the rugged individual was fraught with competition, protection, fear of unworthiness. It was bound up in ego. The new is grateful for the deep listening and gentle feedback that helps me clarify and choose and find first steps. And I'm just as grateful for the involvement in Margaret's journey through listening, feedback, and encouragement. Our two journeys are unique and individual, and at the same time very closely related, impacted by each other. We are traveling together on our two paths.

Through hearing and helping her struggle, my love for her grows. I become more invested in seeing her outcome materialize. I keep hands off the process and the outcome itself so as not to alter her reading of the call. The image that comes to mind is the sport of curling where someone bowls a stone disk, called a "stone," toward the far end of an ice rink and a teammate sweeps the path in front of the stone, careful not to touch it in the process. I sweep her path, and she mine. This new style of spirituality brings me out of the cloister with its aching solitude and separation from the world.

In framing the task of our relationship in spiritual terms we've learned how to love each other, how to translate our love into concrete forms that speak directly to the other's need. I know a very loving man who buys his wife a ring every year until by now there's no way she could ever wear them all. She started out loving the beauty and the symbolism of the rings. He started out knowing it would please her. But without the deep sharing of their soul's journeys they no longer know how to fill each other's heart's desire.

The most important filling of each other's heart's desire comes in the tiny, everyday gifts that flow from seeing the other well.

CHAPTER SEVEN

The Body Flees

The Body Flees

Haunted

I've been haunted by the thought of "who cares?" Who cares about all this stuff, besides me, that is. All the writing gurus say "know your audience" and, presumably, write to their interests or questions. Well, this isn't a passing on of family lore for the new grandchild or somesuch. It's an old woman prattling on in ways that used to bore me to death.

If I have a message it's so simple and obvious it turns to—what? I'm spinning gold into straw. Tote wood, carry water. Thich Nhat Hanh has a simple message too, but it carries weight because it comes from elsewhere, not only from Vietnam but from years of strict discipline in a monastery. My message comes out of the '60s and out of gay pride.

It comes out of the interface between my unique upbringing and my plunging headlong into our culture. Mine was the melting pot era, which strove to demonstrate how American we all were in spite of different backgrounds. The old World War II movies threw together Italian Brooklynites and Appalachian moonshiners and they all stood together against the Hun.

I hid most of my uniqueness from the time I left my childhood stomping grounds, and it was a scramble to find out what was expected and copy it before being indelibly labeled as strange. I was smart enough to hang with a group of unique individuals—oddballs, all—and all struggling to understand what of their uniqueness was acceptable and what needed replacing or smoothing over.

So let's say that my spiritual discipline comes out of the interface between the unique culture of my family and personality and experiences on the one hand, and the culture and times around me on the other.

It's not just that I went through the '60s participating, but that I went through as a bisexual Quaker mystical artist. Can we integrate the parts of ourselves and stay so true to that shifting, elusive self that we can make a spiritual discipline all our own out of it? I'm determined to discover mine now, and so these stories.

We Too Are Part of God

Apollo Coehlo says, "The universe conspires to support the dreamer." That has been true for me. I think dreamers are so important because they are the priests and oracles who can hear the divine message and transmit it to the world. That dreamer within us, who sees us clearly and objectively, isn't that also that of God within? It also speaks to us clearly and objectively, in its own language, which is symbolic, coded, in need of pondering and translating and applying to one's life—much like a mystical experience. These messages need listening to not by the brain, but by the heart. The messages have the ability to open us up, slow us down, give us the courage to act on the promptings of our own conscience, to make us tender toward others. They can transform us.

The hero's journey includes time alone in the wider world, in nature. Whenever we spend time listening to the natural world alone we are close to God. This world is God's body as much as we are. At the last stage of life we see the world in its exquisite beauty—God made visible. What a gift it is and has been, as much as it's given us pain and struggle. One new leaf on a struggling houseplant, the antics of a stray kitten, the bird who comes to eat our humble offering—let alone the kind hospice nurse— are all gifts of God that can fill our hearts. We are one family with all of creation. We can see *out there* as God, then when we find ourselves one with that, we discover that we too are part of God.

It's very hard to take in these realizations on faith. It all becomes a philosophical debate, with good reasons needed to sway us one way or the other. George Fox calls this whole approach "airy notions." What we all need is the *experience*. Of course, we're not in control of whether that happens to us or not. It's a moment of Grace, given to us unexpectedly. I'm tempted to say we need quiet, nature, meditation, soul searching. I do believe these prepare us, but they still don't trigger the experience itself.

I have spent much of my life racing around accomplishing a massive amount of stuff, through double-tasking, scheduling my days very tightly, taking on everything that seemed necessary. It was in the times I was stopped cold by cancer, or dropped everything to be with my parents as they approached death, that I could see that much of that other activity was arbitrary. I did have choices where I'd thought I had none. I did place value on mulling things over, but I allotted time to it on the world's schedule, during vacations when those were possible, rather than when I needed to stop something wrong or make a tough decision. When I really needed to change course I would get sick. In spite of all that, God has poked through now and then.

Nearing Death

These days I spend much of my time in a comfortable recliner that has a breath-taking view of the Puget Sound and the Olympic Mountains. I'm tethered to a machine that feeds extra oxygen to my nose. I'm about thirty pounds lighter than usual and my skin hangs on me like a ninety-year-old. I'm surrounded by books and my computer, the tools I most want now. Earlier I brought out a little table and some clay for a month or two of blissful sculpting.

I'm in that unique state of knowing my life is very limited now and being handily retired and situated so that I can ask questions like, "What am I supposed to be doing right now?" I can prepare for my death.

I am not afraid. When I told that to one young woman, she said, "But how can that be?" That's part of my musings now. It's not a simple answer, but I want to tug out all the strands and weave the whole picture.

I wondered if I was simply in denial, but my dreams make sure I face what's going on. In one, I was a passenger in a car that was navigating a precipitous mountain road. The driver wanted to impress me with his business plan so I would invest in it. He was talking of his future headquarters in the valley far below. He kept gesturing and inadvertently allowing the car to swerve dangerously close to the edge, even catching the wheels on my side in the dirt. I feared for my life and wondered when to grab the wheel out of his hands. I was thinking there was no chance I'd invest in him because he couldn't keep his attention on the task at hand. And then the unthinkable happened. He steered a very loose curve where the road was in a tight curve. We sailed off the side of the cliff. I flew free of the car, down toward my certain death hollering, "Nooooooo!"

While it's true I'm not afraid, that doesn't mean I'm ready to go, or happy to go. My partner and I designed and built our dream home away from the bustle and smog of the city; my daughter is about to give me a first grandchild; I have fascinating projects prepared and ready for this time; my home life is peaceful and happy. Everything is prepared for my final twenty years or so, and now I'll be lucky to get two. Too soon; that's too soon!

I've had friends ask me if I shake my fist at God. I did live with "Rage, rage against the dying of the light!" running through my mind for several days. But my raging is not at God. We are so sheltered from death that we feel entitled to a long life. I read a lot of history, and all eras before ours had so much death that everyone knew grieving intimately. Families lost their children to smallpox and influenza; husbands lost their wives in childbirth; many died from mysterious fevers and fluxes. Doctors stood helplessly by for much of this.

And now, in spite of our bluster, much of our disease process is still a mystery. I've made it through two kinds of cancer to find now that those treatments have saved me from the cancer, but in the process are killing me. My diagnosis is pulmonary fibrosis, with a second auto-immune disease accompanying it, polymyositis, a wasting away of muscle tissue. The pulmonary fibrosis is a progressive encrusting of my lungs with scar tissue until I can't breathe any more. It comes from my immune system not recognizing the cells as mine, or, perhaps, as lung tissue, and so they attack the stranger within.

In 1991 I was diagnosed with Hodgkin's lymphoma. I underwent two surgeries, one to remove a fist-sized tumor from my chest and the other to remove my spleen and check for metastasis in the abdomen. Then began a period of massive radiation treatments to my entire torso. This regimen was standard protocol at the time. I couldn't get anyone to question it or discuss modified versions of it. Now oncologists shake their heads and say, "Oh, we don't do that any more." The radiation oncologist told me my lungs sounded terrible and looked terrible on the x-ray and advised me I should tell doctors and radiologists in the future that I'd had radiation treatments and not to worry about it.

In 2001 I was diagnosed with a particularly virulent kind of breast cancer, almost certainly caused by the radiation treatments. I had a mastectomy and then several rounds of chemotherapy, the standard protocol once again. The chemo made my lungs hurt and function very poorly, especially the final chemo drug, Herceptin. On two of the chemotherapies I asked to stop early. A few months after stopping Herceptin my health started to plummet. I ordered oxygen to help me get around and recover from activities as mild as walking and standing. I found that my oxygen saturation dropped to 74 (100 is normal, 92 or less very impairing) with a short, brisk walk. That summer I lost 25 pounds.

The terminal diagnosis of pulmonary fibrosis shook me seriously, no hope of recovery. My decline was so rapid that we wondered whether I had years or just months to live. A specialist told me that I'd been living with it since the radiation treatments in 1991, and that the chemo had exacerbated it into its present state.

I researched alternative therapies and visited my longtime Chinese acupuncturist and my homeopath. I sought treatment from a naturopath and from my partner, who is an osteopath. There were many approaches to softening the scar tissue in my lungs, and I did them all. At the time of this writing, I breathe more deeply and easily; I have more energy for walking around, talking and doing for myself; I'm using less supplemental oxygen; my weight loss has slowed, and my spirits are bright and optimistic. I look forward to the next pulmonary function test with great curiosity.

As you can hear, I do shake my fist, but not at God. An MD told me to beware of the alternative therapies. They may make me feel better with a placebo effect, but they may do me harm because they haven't been adequately tested. Ah, the irony! I was given the standard protocol, which upon further testing was shown to be overkill. The radiation and the chemo were an attempt to lower my odds of recurrence and metastasis, from 30% to something like 15%. The price was 100% terminal. Whose therapy "May do me harm because of inadequate testing?" By contrast, Chinese acupuncture and herbs have been around for 5,000 years doing no harm and gaining in sophistication and finesse.

I do climb onto a soap box and shake my fist every now and then, but otherwise I find it a waste of time and energy. There are so many important directions for me to pursue. And out my window is that spectacular reminder of the beauty of this world. I watch the storms beat against the house, the fog shroud the far hills in bands, the snow-capped mountains peek through the clouds and catch the morning light, the eagles drop from their watching posts and glide down to fish in the water. What a gift this time on Earth is.

And what a gift it is to have the time for closure in my life. If I were dropped by a massive heart attack or run down by a truck, I wouldn't have the leisure to pull the threads of my life together, to try to make sense of it all, to say goodbye to my loved ones. This is the task at hand for me now.

My first thought for the task at hand was to finish all my unfinished projects. What an exhausting thought that is! My eyes have always been bigger than my stomach when it comes to fascinating projects, and my house is littered with the beginnings of them. I am my mother's daughter. Her house was crammed with the detritus of abandoned projects.

And here I am with my file drawers full of the accomplishments of my varied life, and full of the beginnings of projects that seemed like a good idea at the time. I'm looking for someone eager to take them on, and I know most will end up in the dumpster. Those projects from several decades ago?—I can already see their dumpster-worthiness.

What is important now is not the same as at any other time in my life. So I have to let go of preconceptions and listen closely to what my heart wants to do. It wants to make sense of my life, and that's what this writing is about. That's also why I treasure the visits from loved ones from all the decades of my life, and treasure their view of me, their expression of my gift to them. What are the gifts I've strewn carelessly behind me? They certainly go beyond anything I intended.

I once worked as a substitute teacher at the middle and high school levels. I was often sent into classrooms where I knew nothing about the subject. One such was a girls gym class doing basketball. I'd never even played it. So I set the leaders and stars to organizing and running the practice while I sat on the bleachers with a girl suffering bad menstrual cramps. I can't remember what we talked about. I was probably relaxed and open, and talking with her as an equal. More than a year later she saw me in the grocery store and greeted me with elation. She asked me to wait while she found her mother and brought her to meet me, saying "This is the teacher I told you about!"

What happened there? Certainly nothing I was intending. Perhaps some of the Divine Love we all carry about shone onto her because I wasn't getting in the way of it. We often forget that our primary job in life is this carrying around of the Light, and offering it our hands, and our tongue. We carry it whether we're aware of it or not, and it is often at work without our noticing it.

Quakers put great emphasis on the Light within, that is, in us, but not of us. I've always pictured it as a candle, quite easy to hide under a bushel. One time in my twenties I was accompanying a friend to the airport to pick up her visiting mother. She was nervous and afraid it wouldn't go well, and thought my presence might help. She is a strikingly beautiful woman. I enjoyed watching people's reactions to her as we went about together; I was rarely noticed at all.

This time, though, pushing through the throngs leaving the plane, it was me people were staring at, not her. I was baffled. I even glanced behind me and saw someone turning to continue watching me. I decided to hide, and I knew very well how to blend into the woodwork. I dipped my face to watch my feet while walking, but it dipped into a brilliant golden sun streaming out of my chest. I stumbled and thought I'd better return to normal reality. I pulled my head up, out of the Light and told myself to remember that this really happened. Don't dismiss it later as some kind of hallucination. I never told my friend. I successfully greeted her mother and got them settled back at my friend's house. At home, alone I shook my head and realized I'd underestimated the Inner Light by a wide margin.

The job at hand now is to become more transparent, to allow the Light to shine through me however it will. But I'm bothered by the notion of transparent. I'm not sure I can remove myself, or even *should* remove myself. I've always valued the crusty characters in my life who are totally themselves. And I've been unsatisfied by conversations with New Age-type people who leave me wondering where and what their real truth is. I'm afraid any attempt at transparency would take me to that New Age place.

So perhaps my task is to become as thoroughly myself as I can. Already I've given up on personal aesthetics: hair styling and eyebrow enhancement take too much energy and muscle. It's been a real lesson to come face to face with my vanity and let it go. Take me as I am. It just gets uglier from here, especially at the end. And let loose with the sass and humor. And when the tears come in the middle of a sentence, speak on through them without apology. There are many topics of conversation that are very fragile for me, and those are the most important to explore. If I avoided them neither I nor my friends would find the conversations of value. I am raw naked honest right now, in that most important state of hearing things come out of my mouth that are news to me.

Healthy or Sick, Who Am I?

This morning I dreamed I was buying and fixing up a gorgeous retreat center. It had a sick man living in a basement room who was going to have to go. I went down to speak to him and found his room reeked from a stopped-up toilet. He agreed to go. I agreed to help him with the toilet. I filled a bucket with the shit and headed out to bury it somewhere on the beautiful grounds.

How long has he been living there, deep within me? When I was ten, all the other females in the family came down with polio. I was the healthy one, carrying trays to everyone bunked out in the living room. My four-year-old sister with the raging fever did not die as they had expected. My mother also recovered in good time. My older sister, Mary, lay paralyzed from the waist down for the next year. She'd been a ballet dancer. She hung her toe shoes on the wall at the foot of her bed. We got her a canary. The whole township pulled together to buy her a TV. I brought change in to school one day to put in a jar on the teacher's desk—for "someone in need"—and heard whispers behind me. I knew later that my classmates had known that the someone was Mary.

This was 1950 and polio seemed to be everywhere. Another young ballerina died of it. We knew someone in an iron lung. Richard McFeely, the Quaker headmaster at George School, like President Roosevelt, labored along on polio crutches. We didn't know what to expect for Mary.

She and I grew very close that year. I climbed onto her big bed and learned teenage girl talk a bit early. She was thirteen. Mother and I carried her to the bathtub and massaged her legs. My brother Bill, usually her constant companion, was off at George School. Mary was my first best friend. She recovered the use of her legs and went off to the Quaker school herself the next year.

When I went to George School myself a few years later, Mary and Bill were both gone. What a struggle it was to catch up academically. How socially inept I felt. I was the poor country mouse among rich city mice. I put $5 into my little bank account for the year and drew off it a dollar at a time. The girl in front of me in line once put in $100. Was that for the month, I wondered? For the *week*? I struggled as a junior with all the issues others had dealt with as freshmen: homesickness, inadequacies, dorm life, study habits. When things overwhelmed me, I got sick.

What a relief it was to rest abed in the infirmary. Assignments got an automatic extension. The strain of socializing with girls I didn't understand ceased in that heavenly solitude. I knew and loved solitude. I'd found a way to step out of the rat race for a while and feed my soul. After a bit of a break the gastritis and colitis eased up and I went back into the fray.

In college I didn't feel inadequate or socially inferior, but I still got overwhelmed now and then. When sickness didn't accommodate me with an excuse for a break, I faked it and took a break anyway. My self-image got confused between the "healthy one" and the "sick one."

In the first year of my teaching career I was commandeered into service directing the music department's annual musical. I didn't like the idea. After all, I'd spent my college years directing the music department's musicals, and now I longed for more challenging projects. I even had a script idea pushing its way through to consciousness. I pleaded with them to change from their musical, which I hated, to one—the only one?—that I liked. They agreed. I still feared the strong personalities of the music department and their influence on my new, potentially ideal job.

The script kept forming itself. If I'd been able, I would have laid down all my other obligations and written it. One day I took a bite out of a student friend's hamburger. He came down with hepatitis. I came down with hepatitis. I could hardly drag myself out to the kitchen and the bathtub. I sent my regrets to the music department and my classes and laid back to let the images of the new play roll out. That became the major play I produced that year. It was illness that allowed me to stop going in the wrong direction, shift gears, check the map, and head in the right direction. My other major illnesses also corresponded with major life changes.

And now, here I am, the survivor of three cancers, but succumbing to a supposedly terminal disease. Is there a lesson here? Is it "be careful what you ask for"? Is there a major life change I can't see yet, but if I could, I could make the change and get on with my life? This handy little device within that lets me retreat and ponder, does it have to be illness? Can't I substitute something else? Can I really get the sick man in the basement to move out? Would that make me not sick any more?

This is, after all, the biggest retreat for reevaluation I've ever done. I'm looking not only at my present circumstances, but at my whole life, and with an urgency to get about whatever it is I want to have done. What has this life been for? I don't have the usual Quaker biography of good works, or even the usual artistic biography of published and produced works. I have had some unique experiences of being washed in the Light, carrying the Light, and revealing the Light. I think all else has been secondary to that. Perhaps illness has given me a way to return to that deep guidance at the critical points in my life. Perhaps illness brings me closer to the Light.

This month has been full of dreams of joy, freedom, centered peacefulness. The struggle is gone. I feel close to the Light, even as I feel further from the clutches of death. The medical tests show good news, improved dramatically over a few months ago. But in my dreams I feel closer to the peacefulness of death. In one, my friends didn't recognize me—like Christ on the road to Damascus. I was walking around with my cannula not attached to any oxygen tank. Perhaps I didn't need it any more. It didn't seem to matter which side of death I was on. The solidness of my body and this world are growing thin, as much as I treasure my beloved family and friends and the spectacular piece of the world that lies outside my window. They grow thin at the same time that I feel hope for a longer life. This must be the new change this illness is calling me toward.

Get a Life!

After all my strutting and bragging, I'm back to weak and out of breath. This is a roller-coaster ride. Not only do I swing ecstatically to health and optimism for a long life, but Margaret swings with me. And with the health updates going out, hundreds of distant friends swing too. It's time I put more than my current state of health into those notes. What's my inner struggle? Do I simply throw the idea of death out the window, thank you very much?

Like Margaret, I need to get a life! Yes, some is writing this, but the drive to write faded when my health returned to a better place. No deadline. No motivation.

And what beyond the writing, which after all is still self-obsessed? Yesterday I told Margaret I was going to sit with the Women in Black, and she eagerly joined me. It was a very good experience. I want to become a regular. I spent a lot of time spreading consciousness and courage over the commuters. Then I counted responses and found one in ten or better gave us a sign of solidarity. In the hour and a half, I only saw five expressions of disapproval.

And what else? My urge is finally to get active, after all these years. MoveOn, etc., are often looking for living room screenings. Here I am with a big-screen TV and good DVD player and large living room. And the ability to lead a discussion. We need to find a way to settle lots of people in with less hauling of the heavy couch than we've had. And we need to get people to wash up and not bring germs into the house.

And beyond that? Maybe something up at the hospital about facing death? Wouldn't I need some hospital chaplaincy training or something? Wouldn't I botch it terribly, at least for a while until I knew what I was doing?

And here I go proposing something for others I really need for myself. What I don't have. Which is a live spiritual life. Where is my openness to the flooding Love and Light that I know is there? "If you would know God, go to where the need is greatest and fill it," said those early Quaker missionaries. I'm not filling others' needs, I'm sitting here like a fat toad accepting others' offerings of food, etc. Not a pleasant sight, especially over the long haul. I've been seeing that pattern in my health updates vaguely, as in the far distance, without knowing what to do about it exactly.

I read a good book called *Good Heavens* by Margaret Graham about a poor and uneducated Southern evangelical who withstands the buffets of ridicule with grace and very human muttering. She sticks to her guns about what she perceives as the right thing to do, and ends up transforming a drug rehabilitation home, touching each person there. She alone doesn't do it. She allows the Spirit to work through her. She brings people to Christ and leaves them there, like George Fox! I found myself uncomfortable with the fundamentalist language and attitudes (such as, gays should be celibate) and moved at the same time. She herself was a Christ-like figure.

The time when I was teaching high school, after my cluster college closed, was a difficult time for me. I was a terrible high school teacher. I couldn't make the adjustment to younger people. In fact, the junior and senior classes fared better than the younger ones. I could introduce them to seminar structure and have them teach each other, prepare them for college. But in general I was lame and my classes were out of control. I admired my colleagues, and for the life of me I couldn't learn what I needed from them.

Out of this agonizing time one student stood out. Laurie was radically different from her peers—awkward, bright, theatrical in a clownish way. She didn't date or experiment with makeup. She had few friends she could relax around, though she insisted on some level of friendship, acceptance, fun with everyone there. She roped me into playing the Red Queen to her Alice once, and dressed me in a red chenille bathrobe and a crown from Burger King. She still remarks on her surprise at this modest, quiet Quaker teacher filling the room effortlessly with empirical commands. She says if I could empathize to that degree I surely could empathize with her. Well I did empathize with her, and I don't think I've ever told her that the rest is part of me. I am the Red Queen, and Alice, and on and on. Theater teaches a person that. And how tiresome it is to be stuck in any one of those personalities.

Laurie and I have stayed in touch over the years. She, much to my surprise, has become an Episcopal priest, a lesbian Episcopal priest no less. She now has two small children and a long-term partner she's very happy with. She settled in Hoboken, New Jersey, and started working with the children in the Projects. She found dirt to make a garden with them. Then she started working on a community center, facing all the zoning and funding hurdles that would be way beyond me. That building now stands and is staffed and offering programs for her beloved kids.

She is ready for her next challenge. She applied for a small church in a small working-class town and wanted it so much she asked if we'd pray for her during the interview. At 6 AM Margaret and I were sitting up in bed with our tea, focused on her. Actually I focused more on her committee than on her. I encouraged the committee to trust their positive impressions, to remember the sermon she gave them earlier, which I'm sure moved them to tears (as she had moved me when I heard her preach). I told them I knew she was absolutely genuine, there would be no nasty surprises, she wears her whole self on her sleeve. I told them what a gift she had for seeing the beautiful, seeing God in everyone and loving them. No one would fall asleep during her sermons or walk away indifferent from her undertakings. I told them she had the capability to transform their church, perhaps their whole town before she was done.

At her timid request we prayed once again while the committee met to decide. They chose her. She gives us much credit, though she may well have wowed them all on her own, and how many other friends were praying along with us? If there was any power of persuasion coming from me, I would credit it all to how much prayer energy I've been receiving lately. I've been flooded with it, to such an extent that about a month ago in Meeting I felt that I was spilling blessings over onto everyone in the room. If this is like love—actually, if this *is* love—then I'm confident that it does spill over. A person who is newly and deeply in love is absolutely radiant and can warm and lift everyone in the room. Are these prayers focused love? Is hospital chaplaincy focused love? Aren't all of Jesus' lessons about how to love, God's kind of love? And isn't that what I'm drawn to do now? To give love where I can, where it's needed. I have to get out of my recliner to find where it's needed.

Among Quakers? We're pretty well off for the most part. Except maybe for walking our talk. We could be much more pure, and therefore noticeable, than we are. What if we had a testimony against cars, for example. That's no more radical than those early testimonies. Or against meat. Or against paying war taxes. It would at least make us all uncomfortable as hell and aware of our falling short, of "sinning," as that early Quaker said.

We need to learn the delicate art of listening to our conscience and acting on it. It goes beyond what we've experienced or thought about, and stirs us in a direction against the norm. To sin is to fail to act on our conscience. To act on our conscience is to become a social oddball. Yes, many of us join social movements after they've become socially acceptable, and so avoid the oddball stage. But aren't we all designed to reveal a tiny bit of God's Truth? What is that tiny bit for me? For you?

Here's another way to know God, along with finding a need and filling it. Act on your conscience. Well, so I've identified two great-sounding paths that I don't tread! Ha! So, what do I do, if anything? (Maybe this is why my spiritual life is dried up.) My sister Mary answers every call, no matter how faint, from others (not necessarily from herself). She admires the brilliant color of a poor woman's coat in the post office; she listens to the Alzheimer's patient who is making no sense and says, "Tell me more." She reaches out in simple friendship, much as our mother did. Another path I haven't trod! It's so hard to see what I do by comparing what others do.

And so I ask how I've impacted others. I'd do better by impacting others any way I can see, right now. Or maybe even focusing on my impact is self-obsessed. I need to listen to God. Where am I nudged to go? What am I nudged to stop doing, to do? And then do it with courage, with the best of intentions, whether skilled or not. Do it with love.

Medical Rant

Yesterday a friend told me of one of her friends who'd been sent home to die within a few months by his doctor. That was twenty-two years ago, and he's doing fine, thanks to a vigorous regimen of alternative medicine. I seem to hear a lot of these stories, more than I used to before my own illness. Of course they're meant to give me hope, and they do. Of course they're "only anecdotal," the excuse for dismissing them because they don't fit the physician's worldview.

Why must doctors say, "There's nothing that can be done," when they really should be saying, "We don't know anything else to do for you"? Why don't doctors pay attention when you tell them what you're doing on your own that seems to be working? My doctor reports to me that an old patient is still alive ten years later and off oxygen. When I ask if that person is doing any alternative medicine, she doesn't know! She then writes a report up on me that says I'm responding well to her steroid and chemo regimen, taking credit for my improvement with no official mention of my other treatments.

It's a self-fulfilling prophecy. Of course it seems there's nothing to be done if you refuse to look at what's being done.

There are many things we can't prove to the standards the FDA demands. Those standards really only fit pills anyway, but they're used to block serious consideration of many things. Pediatricians refuse to run double-blind experiments to prove beyond a doubt that breastfeeding is immensely healthier than formula. The reason is that they'd have to ask half the women to withhold breastfeeding in place of formula, and they know enough to find that unethical and injurious to the infants' health.

We know enough that we don't have to know more. But in the meantime, the formula lobby managed to get strong breastfeeding ads yanked and toned down to the point of ineffectiveness, because there was no "acceptable" proof.

Held in Love

The more we let our guard down and the closer we look at each other, the more we love each other. What a hard lesson to learn, that love is lost in hiding and faking, and found in revealing our hapless and humble truth. God loves us as we are, and incredibly, so do our dearest friends.

Margaret and I sat in a hot tub and spoke of death, our tears creeping down. We spoke of being afraid and not being afraid, of our great sadness at being cheated out of our last decades together. One would think I have the bigger challenge, but I disagree. I will return to that loving Presence, while she will grieve. Between now and then lie years (we hope) of one-sided caretaking. While still working, she has shouldered all the jobs I used to do for us, and added to it my home healthcare. I seek out ways to support her that take little muscle: editing her writings, doing her accounting, guiding her through the maze of her computer. She is tireless, patient, and willing. I stand humbled by her love.

One time while Margaret was working, my ride to the doctor in town fell through. I called several neighbors who'd offered to help, but it was one of those days when people weren't available. Each unproductive call made the next call harder. I felt a helpless panic begin to rise. In spite of abundant evidence to the contrary, I felt more and more alone and unloved. While I did find a ride in time, that experience left me shaken by the extent of my need. I've always been proud of my independence and naïve about the extent of others' help. Now there was no escaping how big a burden I was, especially on Margaret.

Thank goodness for our care committee who walk this path with us, who share in our grief and our traumas. When we meet, everyone speaks of individual struggles and milestones, and this cheering and grieving for each other has become the most important part of our gatherings. They do bring enough food for us to live off the leftovers for a while. They occasionally tackle fixing the sink or sewing up my lap robe that very evening. They watch to see that our garbage can is out on Tuesday morning. They pour as much love and care into Margaret and into each other as into me, which makes me feel less like a drain on them. We laugh and cry and sometimes get so boisterous I'm exhausted, and I love it.

Often the truth pops out in this boisterous joking better than in quiet introspection. When planning a car vacation with two friends, we were juggling my required encumbrances—wheelchair, folding recliner, plug-in oxygen concentrator, and a trunk full of oxygen tanks. But, I worried wouldn't these tanks become a bomb if we were rear-ended? Soon we had me towed in the wheelchair behind the car to make everything fit. Then my lap was full of oxygen tanks, so those in the car would not be endangered. The rear-ending would send me off with a blast of glory! None of those messy, lingering deaths for me.

I am overflowing with the blessings of all these friends from my long life. So overflowing that I've been practicing sending concentrated streams of blessings to others who ask. I've never been big on intercessory prayer, never knelt by the bed to say, "God bless Mommy and Daddy and…" But now, when my priest friend falls in love with a parish and wants to be assigned there, I spend the time of her interview helping the elders see her clearly, and helping her relax and be herself. I hope this constitutes a blessing.

I'm finding the miracle of love, how it multiplies as one gives it away and as one lets it in. If death is no longer the ultimate threat, then there really is nothing to be afraid of, and with nothing to fear, love flows freely. What is more important than my helping my partner bring her gifts forth? I have talents useful for her, as she has for me. What is more valuable in this life than helping each other up?

Of course, I can say this from my fortunate position of retirement. I can treasure this most valuable possession: time. I can savor my chosen activities like a fine meal. I can spend the entire hour of a friend's surgery being present for it.

I'm Nobody, Who Are You?

I slept deep and hard last night, perhaps because the care committee met and evoked a new reality check for me, maybe for me and Margaret. At least it prompted me to speak out loud what was festering behind the face of things.

I wrote a new health update a couple of weeks ago. That was my first admission of reality. But since then I've dutifully taken my antibiotic and anti-inflammatory, which should have addressed the acute possibilities— bronchitis and pleurisy. Those symptoms are the same. What's left is the conclusion that my condition is now this much worse. Or the unknown, which modern Western medicine isn't good at admitting.

So I've been taking my other cures as well, prayer from those friends who are so good at that, much better than I. The health letter openly asked for that.

What I'm feeling is a mixture of fear, urgency, and sadness. What is this urgency to express all the things I've been procrastinating about almost my whole life? I am more than the crumbs I'll be leaving behind. There have been such symphonies of creativity within me, and what's made it into the world is such a squeak. Here I thought I'd gotten over my grandiosity.

I want to fully realize the potential of my inner symphonies, and maybe it takes a terminal disease, the threat of absolutely no more time, to tackle these shibboleths. Isn't this the grandmother of all deadlines? Now or never, kiddo. If you procrastinate any more, then that's your legacy. "Here's Lynn, she lived a quiet life, full of potential."

But you know, I'd really like to leave a play behind that people want to produce after I'm gone. I want to provoke questions and original thought with an exhibition of naked ladies. I like that my ex-students, now mature professionals themselves, have incorporated some of my ideas and techniques into their work. These are also my children. A bit of me will travel into the future. This is what I want. Not glory during my life. Lord knows, I've worked hard to prevent that, to be able to live a quiet life out of the spotlight.

I've pulled out *The Dream* because it keeps returning to me. It's missing a major scene (or act) that I couldn't write before. Did I run out of time, or understanding, or images? Now I know what needs to go there. The question is, can I still crank out a dramatic scene full of shocking imagery and grab-you-by-the-throat truth?

Lurking behind that project is the deck of Tarot cards, which could be completed now with a lifespan of images, where before was only youth. My current projects need completing, too: the video, these pages now possibly with illustrations, the naked ladies crowding the shelves. The naked ladies who are taking me somewhere unknown.

These painful lungs are a wake-up call. The hero of spontaneous healing just may not gallop in at the last minute and rescue me. My unusually stable last couple of years may not signal a turnaround toward health and another few decades of life. It is, after all, the nature of this disease to progress into more painful, less efficient lungs. At least that's the Western medicine view of it. And it's supported by lots of patients fulfilling the prediction.

I'll talk with Dr. Xie, my Chinese Medicine doctor, again about her prophecy that I'll heal. What is the nature of that absolute belief that triggers spontaneous healing? Am I being defeated by my own healthy skepticism? Not so healthy, then, eh? We wanted to restart the Tibetan monks on another year of prayer. I'm not too skeptical to do that. They must know things about prayer that we can't even guess at.

I'm skeptical of the Western newcomers just as I wouldn't trust my acupuncture to a young, Western-trained naturopath. That would be like asking a craniosacral therapist to do the work of an osteopath. That's like the men out there giving workshops to women on the women's wisdom they are finally uncovering in themselves (or in their wives). Let the wives give the workshops. Let the men listen and learn.

I spent far too many years feeling I had to have the answers. To be a professor is to step into the role of Man of Authority. I see now how severely that limited my helpfulness. How I wanted the authority men had, simply by nature of their gender. How hard it was to learn the trap that authority was. How much it kept me from really listening, not only to the other person, but also to the responses that floated in from the greater wisdom.

It's hard to listen like that because we've all suffered years of condescending, patronizing responses from people who feed on vulnerability. They're delighted to find someone humble so they can be one-up. I've spent years perfecting ways to cut through that condescension, to shock them with what I do know, to work them closer to a relationship of equals. It's very hard work. Who'd want to invite that by approaching with an attitude of Emily Dickinson's "I'm nobody, who are you?"

Setbacks

This is a hard time. After two years of holding steady, I find myself significantly worse. Very painful lungs and much weakness in my body. The pulmonologist says ruefully, "Sorry, I have nothing more to offer." Strong pain meds, which I'm not ready for yet!

Meanwhile, my brother, with cheerful optimism, gathers a healing circle, and many others are holding me in the light. I'm reading *The Intention Experiment* and seeing that, yes, the lab experiments prove that mind can control matter, and yet, I still don't know how to participate effectively in my own healing. In fact, do I really believe that "my healing" is a genuine possibility? The best I got during that long respite was "I can live with this level of disability—roll my tank around and still do most of what I want."

Now I try to include the same errands and chores and exciting activities that I did a month ago, and I'm a basket case afterwards. I read back over my calendar at all I've been trying to cram into my life. Whatever happened to the long stretches of time and contemplation and appreciation of this world?

I'm close to finishing some of my projects, like my video on Stone Age art and culture, and that pushes me. I want to take and exhibit my Stone Age ladies at Yearly Meeting, and *that* pushes me. The ladies continue to push me to understand their lesson, and so I read. And I've somehow, and to some unknown degree, taken on the making of a video of our 102-year-old friend Maurine before she dies, preferably, and that pushes me.

I have a faith that this pull into the future will keep me alive. The other day my friend Lawrene paraphrased Jung, saying, as long as you serve God, God will keep you around (in some such words). That's the conclusion I've been coming to myself. Though some people serve God by giving their lives, like Mary Dyer and Martin Luther King Jr., my death will not make a stir. It's only my life that might—my works.

I wonder if I get worse when I drift off course. I'm getting worse, whether I'm on or off course. Perhaps I need the reminders of the looming deadline to keep me on course, keep me moving, questing, producing. Perhaps I have plenty of time as long as I use it well. Now I'm going to feel guilty every time I relax with a Sudoku!

We each have our tiny little plot of heaven. My friend Bill's wisdom is in gratitude. Can I remember to stop and be grateful many times a day for what I've been given, and not whine for more? What I've been given is so much more than most have! Love. Beauty. Time. Tools. Talent. Vision. All this above and beyond my basic needs, and even these special needs. There's food in the freezer. There's enough money to go to the dentist. There are loved ones at the other end of the phone and computer. There's my nearest and dearest love walking this hard path with me. How did I ever get so blessed?

The scene from *Oliver* comes to mind: "Please, sir, can I have some more?" Can I now be given my health back? The long sunset years of my life back? What would I have to do to deserve that?

These naked ladies are part, at least, of the answer. Along with their form must come some understanding of their meaning. Something big from that matriarchal time is coming through to now, something that mingles with all the rest that has been coming through. I've had to catch up with the feminist thinking and the Goddess scholarship of the last 25 to 30 years. But I've also had to listen directly to these figures and what they bring with them. "What canst *thou* say?"

It is falling together very slowly, slowly enough for me to distinguish between my intellectual excitement and the deep chime of an emotional chord struck. I'm often in territory that has no words yet. What feels big sounds trite when I try to explain it. These are the Great Mother (many say so), who is also Mother Earth (what else is new?). It takes reading of some scientific guy with a theory of the nesting of all things, to give the mystical truisms the respectability of the scientific world. Maybe this really does describe the shape of things. Maybe the basic shape of the universe is female after all.

My latest dream is about the shutting down of an underwater archaeological dig. The crew knows there's much more treasure to be found, but the bosses in their corporate headquarters have decided to quit. I've pocketed a tiny green goddess that looked like it was going to be swept up and thrown away. Someone is searching all visitors for loot on the way out, and I have to drop it surreptitiously and hope to get back to pick it up again. I do get back to search, but don't find it, though the crew and a guard dog all accept me as OK to be there.

What does this dream tell me? Can I talk to my own headquarters and convince them to continue the dig? The true wisdom is in the crew, not those holding the purse strings. As my daughter Kindred reminds me, the designers are too detached from the action to know best. It's the carpenters who know what's possible. Unlike her, I've always been aligned with the front office. Now I have to join the crew. Get my hands dirty. Play in the mud.

The books tell me one thing, the clay another. My "front office" persona complained of the expense of baking these pieces in the oven before firing them, and even of firing them on the very slowest setting. And so they've been breaking in the kiln. The boss isn't listening to the crew. How do I get her/him to visit the site, or the studio? How do I get crew onto the board? Get unified?

And on another level, how do I listen to my lungs and not my pulmonology brain? I need an anatomy lesson. I don't know enough detail to really understand how they work, and how they now don't work, how and where the scar tissue is advancing. Experiments on prayer say the more specific the requests, the more effective the results.

Hospice

This is the name of the new stage I've entered. The first shocking meaning is that death is inescapable now. The focus shifts from keeping or restoring health to the lungs to keeping me comfortable. This may be more complex for me. Do I stop going to Seattle for acupuncture? That would really be a sign of defeat. Dr. Xie was my last and most steadfast holdout, insisting I was not dying when all others were talking about how long I had.

Morphine is now a major component in my life. I give myself an additional squirt under the tongue before rising on a shower morning. Otherwise I'm a quivering mass of jelly by the end, back on the bed for recovery.

Death

Death is my companion. Thank goodness for Margaret who is the first to hear my fears and my nightmares. Grief is visible on her heart, but her love flows even more strongly than before the diagnosis, if that's possible.

When I was young my mother had a near-death experience on the operating table. She told me afterwards what she experienced on that journey, my own firsthand account from a source I trusted implicitly. She was drawn to the Light, which filled her with love, bliss. She found herself in a firmament of souls, each an individual star, yet not separate from one another. There was no need to communicate with one another because all were in the One Mind, One Heart. She was reluctantly pulled back into this world.

That image has lived with me the rest of my life, giving me courage to risk all. When my mother was near her own death, well into her 80s, I asked her what she remembered from that experience. She didn't even remember that it had happened. I told it back to her, thinking it might be useful, but it didn't seem to impress her. Perhaps it had become so much a part of her faith that the specifics were irrelevant. I only saw one time when she seemed shaken by the nearness of her own death. She was remarkably calm and concerned for the friends who were coming to see her.

That experience of hers has also become a solid part of my own faith. I've read enough of other near-death experiences to see how consistent they all are. So my challenge is not connected with where I'm headed but with what I must let go of and leave behind. I'm young enough that most of those I love are here, not there. Those I've traveled the longest with— my dear sister Mary and other family members; those I've shared most intimately with—my dear partner, Margaret, and other close friends; those I've given the most labor and heartache to—my dear daughter Kindred; these are the hardest to leave behind.

How can we leave our love here, though the body goes? I know my mother's love is knitted into my every fiber. It is the substrate of my courage and self-acceptance, my caring for others. She's left me that as surely as her genetic material. Mary and I joke about her presence when we hang a slightly used paper towel over the oven handle to dry for another use, or tear a tiny post-it note in half for a short message. Her "ghost" is quirky but very loving. I know she was unusually loving, partly by the report from her two remaining sisters. They characterize themselves—they were the last three for a long time—as, Betty the smart one, Dot the funny one, and Mother the loving one.

I know I'm not as loving as she was. I'm none of those three characterizations. It's very hard to see yourself, and probably a waste of time to try, though—I must say—I'm curious. I'd love to listen in on my own memorial service. Maybe others in the cumulative can make a coherent whole picture where I can't.

What is my unfinished business with those I love? Do I need to make amends? Express things I've never said? Apologize? Appreciate? This is the business I should be about.

Bedridden

I woke up happy this morning. How can that be, after a week of increasing limitations? I fought off the commode because of the image using that conveys. Yet walking to the bathroom stirs the muscles into a fury. As soon as I gave in to the commode I felt the rightness. I'm headed for bedridden, like it or not, and when I accept that, I wake up happy.

In this morning's dream I taught people how to hear speech—even noise—as music, and how to see with new eyes. I made an eye for a friend that was slightly larger and more intense than her other eye. It was quite fragile, though. She had to learn how to blink and look left and right without damaging it. Are these ways of seeing and hearing that come from the other side?

After all this talk of the Gateway through the feminine (birth), I guess it's time to explore the Gateway through Death. Before, I've sat by the bedside; now I'm becoming the bedridden, drifting in and out of consciousness more than usual. I look forward to my dear friend Jay drumming me in and out of consciousness. I don't trust shamanic acts to be as effective as dreams, though perhaps they're more easily applied.

The *Grace in Dying* by Kathleen Darling Singh focuses on the spiritual process triggered by knowing you're close to death. Those of us who have not practiced a spiritual discipline designed to take us to the edge of mystical union—and that might be most of us—are confronted with questions and uncertainty, fear when death is certain. Singh says that the spiritual process is triggered by a nearing death, that we move into and through the process of coming closer to God whether we intend it or not, whether we know how or not.

This gateway is about detaching, as the birth one is about attaching. At the birth end there's a lot of variety in opinions of how and when the soul and the new body merge. Some believe they merge in the final trimester, while others believe three months after birth. On the other end, I'm sure the soul is a part of why a person hangs on until some particular loved one can get there.

The soul carries our larger task. As Florida Scott Maxwell proposed, each of our lifetimes makes us an expert, a master, in something. The most gruesome, hard-trodden life will teach us endurance and patience. This is the gift we have to take back to God. When we return, God's pool of endurance grows larger. This is a revolutionary and important thought. God is not complete and finished. God is growing and evolving along with everything else.

We are part of God's multiple manifestations.

At Home

I slept for eight hours straight last night. How long has it been since I've done that? And what was it that has brought me such a profound sense of safety and peace, so deep that I can lay my vulnerable body into God's loving arms? Have I finally gotten to where I've been stretching toward, or have I simply stopped stretching and accepted *here* as the right place to be?

That long-ago promise, that I would be held in God's love throughout my life, has been fulfilled. I've felt it so many times, in private and through others' tender care, and now I feel it almost constantly. I fall asleep into a soft palm. The end won't be so very different.

Postscript

Lynn took her last breath into that soft palm of God's love on October 31st, 2009. It is fitting that she took her leave from this earthly life on Halloween, her favorite holiday. In her last weeks she offered new titles for some sections of the manuscript and she listened to and commented on parts she remembered that she wanted to edit. She also dictated short pieces she hoped could find a place in her book. Those of us who sat at her bedside recorded much of what she said, and some is included in this postscript. Her mind and spirit were in a place somewhere between the world we know and the world that was beckoning her.

—Margaret

9/20

I woke up one morning feeling a huge amount of peace, calm, which I often feel at nighttime. Night is the time of peace. I started taking my morning regimen, and I felt good to take it. Hard to talk about it because my body is going to enact it, I am afraid. My body suddenly went from peacefulness to something very different. I got nausea and everything that pharmaceuticals are going to give me. Then a booster dose of morphine so I could endure the rigors of getting up. It started with the Prilosec, it was wrongness for my body, a terrible clash. And then it went through that to something else and then to something else, and I was all screwed up. I made the transition from a natural state to the big pharmaceuticals and the best they had to offer. I thought ironically, later, the "solution": the journey from the Paleolithic natural person to the pharma, unnatural person. How do *they* know? They are not in my body. So I decided to try to hold on to the natural as much as I possibly could. I knew I needed to keep using the oxygen because the body reacts too strongly to not having oxygen. All of this happened as I got to the tilting place in the middle of my journal. I have never known what that little middle place marker meant. Would I die? Would it be insignificant? Here I was at the middle of my book and my own decisions on treatment. This feels huge to me—to want to be free and clean and clear and walk forth to meet my maker in a different kind of way. That glorious mother, not my mother, but Mother as Source. It is interesting that people cannot hear God as mother because of their own personal mothers.

9/21

A thought I had in the middle of the night: What if there were no mistakes? If nothing were a mistake? That would mean I never made a mistake. You couldn't get off your path. The bad decisions you make as a twenty-year-old are not mistakes. Our whole religion would collapse like a house of cards because our sins are our mistakes and it's assumed to be very difficult to get back to the straight and narrow. And here I am saying that dancing across the path is more fruitful than following the straight and narrow.

9/27

[Lynn reported her dream]: I cavorted along a path at a summer camp kind of place. I kept going off the path and telling the person with me that it was much more fun to be off the path than on it.

10/11

I have just peeped through to the other side! I see a big spherical object, and if I were to look through it I could see the other side. It is made of concrete, and I am intrigued by how it works, but as I talk about it, it starts to break up. I didn't look through, because I guess I am not ready to go.

10/15

Some tiny thoughts. Things are coming to their essence these days.

I have reduced my diet to decadence. I have reduced my medicine to those that are experiential. My food to the level of deliciousness, quick release of sugars: fruit, not lentils.

That's one of the lessons I'm learning from the young ones. That we should have more fun. Who would have guessed that the true end would be to go out dancing and playing and happy.

As the veil is getting thinner I am conversing more and more with people on the other side. And it is distressing because I think I haven't said anything on this side but people look at me blankly like I have said nonsense. The people I am talking to on the other side are ordinary people. I see people in the room, getting dressed. Stressful things don't matter when the veil is this thin.

There are little pinholes. Little dots of light are all over the place in the corners of the room, in the pages of the paper. They are just there and have been there for a couple of days now.

I feel half here, half there. The whole world is peppered with little lights. It's as if an angel, many holes, different sizes, different size holes.

I almost crossed the threshold four times this week but didn't.

10/17

You have to get one level more conscious about expressing. That's been happening all along for me.

Excuse me, is thee with me? Oh Kindred isn't here. Fragments of people are here sometimes, not all the time.

10/20

Lynn: Did I sign the paper about the garbage?

Margaret: Does thee mean the cremation form?

Lynn: Yes, but the word garbage needs to be on that form. That's what this body is becoming.

10/23

I want to formulate a vision of life on the other side. I've been back and forth enough times that that should be possible to do. First I try a visionary existence, dismissing at the same time.

10/24

I thought it would be good to set up tours from one side to the other side. Not a fun house tour but a serious one. You'd let them learn their own lessons and come back and apply them to their own lives and to know what it is they are to do. Enough for now.

10/26

The moaning wall or the wailing wall, call it the grieving wall instead.

10/29

I came into this state with so few wits I couldn't even keep track of my wits. I had three major categories and one major goal, and I couldn't even keep track of that. I didn't see myself as having tools, I just saw myself as wandering in the void.

I wish I had something solid to stand on. I think the point is to have nothing to stand on in order to get to the other side.

Hold on. Stop everything. [Lynn asked for the care committee to come to her bedside to consult.]

L: I can't reach the tipping point. I've been ready and waiting—quick and dirty. I think that eventually when I take a nap, terribly exhausted, it's a trial—that I will just move to the other side. What is my resistance to leaving?

M: I think thy timing might be perfect. In two days it's Halloween…

L: I'll be the wicked witch. (laughs)

M: . . .when the veil between the worlds is the thinnest of the whole year. Thy leadings have always been perfect, and I trust that thy leading to tipping over to the other side will be perfect too. . .

L: Everything is okay, all is fine. . . My own work left to do in this life is to learn how to love Margaret. . .

M: I have been loved by thee for 16 years and thee will endure forever in my heart.

L: I talk about different layers of love. . .

M: What layer does thee think thee is missing?

L: One of absolute truth. . . I want to test truth on this side of the veil and that's why I have the desire to live.

M: What would help thee feel more complete about that?

L: [Looks at Margaret and says] Hello gorgeous woman, love of my life.

10/30

I own all of 60 pounds. Remember how someone said, "It's a wonder she can move herself around in bed"?

I'd like the room to be full of oxygen. [Lynn had taken the canula off her face awhile before.] Pull the oxygen into the sphere. It's rich. It feels wonderful.

Some day, not too long from now we will be together. That's not a question, not a statement. Don't hurry it. We will let love enter us. That is what it's about. And then we move above and from that comes the job of image. It's absolutely creative, something that we . . . I'm right in the midst.

10/31 1:10 AM [waking from sleep]
L: Is thee awake?

M: Yes.

L: Maybe I can't do anymore. Is that alright?

M: Absolutely, no worries.

L: That's good. I would child's play it if I could. Actually I've been playing it for a month or so.

6:00 AM

L: Where am I?

M: From my perspective thee's at home on Whidbey Island, but I think thee's traveling to the other side. Thee knows more about where thee is than I do.

L: Now I've got it, we're in our room, the room we should be in. We are in our meeting room, where we've been meeting every Friday, where I seem to live. It's a good place to be, the meeting room.

6:45 AM

L: Is there a possibility of lesbian love?

M: Yes.

L: Well, that's nice. I did stay up most of the night and told most of my story. That was an ordeal.

M: Is thee ready to rest now? Is thy story complete?

L: Yes, I guess people heard it.

M: Yes, I heard it. I wrote it down.

10:38 AM

Thought I had a whole thing worked out. Huh. Oh well. I was a lot younger then, earlier in the cycle. I ran the cycle, and I repeated the running of it in each of these open sessions. It's what I've done.

1:23 PM

I guess I crossed. It was a little cruise ship, one for diversion. You paid so much to get on it in the first place. You know, the universeness. Less nervousness there because there's someone to watch. Hey!

2:30 PM
Ob La Di, Ob La Da, Life goes on. . .

4:15 PM
Lynn took her last breath and closed her eyes.

Glossary of Common Quaker Terms

AFSC (American Friends Service Committee) is a Friends service and relief organization that was awarded the Nobel Peace Prize in 1947.

Clearness is when individuals or groups are confident after an inward search that their decision is consistent with God's will.

Conservative Friends are members of the Religious Society of Friends who practice unprogrammed worship and have an explicitly Christ-centered theology.

Continuing Revelation is the belief that God continues to speak to people now; that the Bible is not the final word, but one standard of truth to aid us in a continuing search for truth in our day.

Discernment (individual and corporate) is the individual or group spiritual practice of coming to know God's will for us by prayerfully sifting through what we have heard within, and recognizing and separating it from our fear, pride, ambition, etc.

Mary Dyer (1611-1660) English Quaker who was hanged on the Boston Commons for repeatedly defying a law banning Quakers from the Massachusetts colony.

Margaret Fell (1614-1702) English Friend often credited with the pivotal organizational development of the early Friends movement; traveled widely in the ministry, suffered three imprisonments by the authorities, authored many tracts, including *Women's Speaking Justified*, one of the first justifications ever written by a woman in defense of women's right to participate fully in all aspects of religious life; who later married George Fox.

George Fox (1624-1691) English spiritual seeker whose religious awakening resulted in the formation of the Religious Society of Friends; he traveled widely in the ministry, was married to Margaret Fell, and wrote prolifically despite religious persecution and frequent imprisonment by the authorities.

Friend (interchangeable with Quaker) is the popular name for a member of the Religious Society of Friends. The Society emerged in England as a Christian denomination during the mid-1600s and is now practiced around the world in a variety of forms. The liberal branch of Quakerism is experience-based and non-creedal.

Inner Light (Light Within) is the presence of God in our hearts that illuminates truth and strengthens and guides us. It is sometimes referred to by Friends as the Spirit, the Guide, the Holy, the Spirit of Truth, the Inward Christ, "that of God in every one."

Leading is an inner sense of being led by God to undertake a particular course of action.

Meeting for Worship In the tradition of an unprogrammed or "silent" Friends meeting, worship is without a pastor or pre-arranged program. Friends gather in expectant waiting upon God and the leadings of the Spirit, which may be manifest in vocal messages, prayer, or in silent communion. Many Friends Meetings are programmed, with a pastor and an established order of service.

Monthly, Quarterly, and Yearly Meetings are organized geographically by a calendar nomenclature (monthly, quarterly, yearly) which designates the regularity of their business meetings. Every Friends Meeting is designated as a monthly meeting because it has a (more or less often) monthly meeting to conduct business; quarterly meetings consist of several monthly meetings and meet typically every three months; yearly meetings are made up of several quarterly meetings and meet once a year.

Plain Speech The Religious Society of Friends was founded in mid-seventeenth century England where people were addressed according to their social status. Quakers chose to address everyone using plain speech (thee and thou), as an expression of their belief that we are all equals because God's light shines in us all.

Proceed as Way Opens (Openings) is a phrase referring to Friends practice of waiting for divine guidance, noticing a path ahead and then moving forward.

Quaker is the traditional or popular name of a member of the Religious Society of Friends, which began in England in the 1600s. Friends are known for their outward practices of peace, simplicity, integrity, and equality, which are reflective of their belief that there is that of God in all people. The name "Quaker" was originally a derogatory term given by the Puritans to early Friends who sometimes "quaked" during worship or when giving public testimony.

Queries are questions for reflection based on Friends testimonies, which are read and pondered for spiritual guidance by individuals and by meetings.

Sin is falling out of right relationship with God.

Testimonies are outward practices and attitudes that are reflections of an inward faith. Traditionally the central testimonies include simplicity, peace, integrity, community, and equality.

Way Closed/Way Opened is a phrase referring to Friends practice of waiting for divine guidance, and then moving forward with the faith that God's will and direction will continue to be revealed.

John Woolman (1720–1772) Tailor and journalist best known for his successful travels to witness nonviolently against slavery, to protect the rights of Native Americans, and to recognize the relationship between exploitive economic production and the seeds of war and injustice.

About the Author

Lynn Waddington, a lifelong Quaker, was born in 1940 in rural southern New Jersey and raised in a "19th century childhood." When the '60s came around, she went through participating—as a bisexual Quaker mystical artist. Her early education in one-room schoolhouses was in stark contrast to the academic and personal rigor of the Quaker boarding school she experienced in high school, and in contrast to college, which taught  her much about the downsides of education—lessons that served her well as a college professor of visual and performing arts. As she faced her impending death she wrote about staying true to her path, and she pursued a passion that had possessed her for decades: the art and culture of Paleolithic and Neolithic times. This study prompted her to reproduce many of the hand-held figures of those periods and to produce a video titled *When God Was Female*, completed just months before she died. Lynn's essays have been published in *Enlivened by the Mystery: Quakers and God* and *Held in Love: Life Stories to Inspire Us Through Times of Change*. She maintained her fine sense of humor right to the end.

CPSIA information can be obtained at www.ICGtesting.com
Printed in the USA
BVOW012316170612

292930BV00004B/2/P